Gordon Lamont is a writer, rad
After teaching drama in Notti
worked for Roundabout, the Nottingham Playhouse
Community Company before joining BBC Education as a
producer. During 12 years with the corporation he produced
radio drama, television documentaries and Internet sites. He
was a pioneer in the development of digital radio and also ran
the BBC's Work Life Balance project. In 2003 he left the BBC
to freelance and has developed a successful career running
creative training and development courses for a wide range of
clients as well as contributing to radio training courses for the
BBC. He continues to write and produce radio programmes.

His previous books include *Work–Life Balance* (Sheldon
Press, 2001), co-written with his wife Ronni, and the *BBC
Drama Handbook* for primary teachers (BBC, 1994) with Geoff
Readman.

www.lamonts.org.uk

To Ronni, Claire and Jim who light the way

The Creative Path

Living a More Vibrant Life

Gordon Lamont

First published in Great Britain in 2004 by
Azure
1 Marylebone Road
London NW1 4DU

British Library Cataloguing-in-Publication Data
A catalogue record for this book is available from the British Library

ISBN 1-902694-28-7

1 3 5 7 9 10 8 6 4 2

Typeset by Avocet Typeset, Chilton, Aylesbury, Bucks
Printed in Great Britain by Bookmarque Ltd, Croydon, Surrey

Contents

1 ✦

Starting out on the creative path

In this book I hope to provide inspiration and practical ideas for you to stretch and develop your own creativity, to think and do in different ways. I've tried to write so that the book can be picked up and put down at odd moments, perhaps during a short break from work (in or out of the home), or when travelling. You might find it useful to have a notebook to jot down any ideas that come to you while trying some of the exercises in this book. Apart from that and occasionally some materials, what you chiefly need is something you already have in abundance: your creativity and a willingness to use it.

Why work on creativity?

One of the jobs I do involves teaching radio skills to new recruits for the BBC and one of the clips we play always gets a laugh. It's a vox pop of people talking about what they're thinking 'at the moment'. The last person to speak, when asked what she's thinking at the moment, replies something like, 'Nothing, I've given up thinking. I used to get so stressed thinking about everything, now I don't bother. Life is much more peaceful without thinking.'

What's your reaction to this? Can you empathize with this woman, or do you think she's got it wrong? Can we really stop thinking? I can certainly understand her view. She's a bit tongue in cheek but she has a serious point; there are times when it would be nice to stop thinking. We can all recognize the mental state where the same thoughts go round and round and we lose that sense of just being. Or we just get bored with having the same ideas and reactions all the time. For me, creativity offers a way out of the traps and eddies that we find ourselves caught in; creativity offers a way forward in our thinking. So that might be a reason why you want to work on creativity; to see things in a new way and step out of oft-repeated, dead-end thinking. This might be important for you personally and it might be important for your work situation.

The worst job I ever did was packing yoghurt pots (just the pots, no yoghurt in them) as they came off an injection mould-ing machine. It was the same thing for 12 solidly dull hours every day. Was the job creative? Not in the least. Did I need creativity to get me through? Silly question – I must have lived a hundred different lives, devised a thousand crazy schemes and had just as many weird and wonderful thoughts as those pots fell endlessly off the end of the machine. I've probably never been so creative. That's the mother of invention for you, and it also demonstrates the wonderful human cap-acity to be creative with the most unpromising material. Who'd ever have thought that the deadly dull yoghurt pot factory would provide inspiration for a book on creativity 30 years later?

Another reason why you might want to work on your creativity is that you feel there's something lacking. Perhaps you used to have a creative outlet and you've let it drop for any one of a number of reasons. I hope that this book will give you some fresh impetus to integrate creative thinking and action into your life. It won't directly help you to take up a pottery or dance class if that's the sort of creativity you're missing, but it might help you to recognize and exercise your creative gifts and perhaps give you the stimulus you need to get clay on your hands or dance shoes on your feet again.

You might have a specific project or issue that you want to work on more creatively. This might be a film script, or a relationship issue, or work-life balance, or changing your diet, or any one of a zillion things that might need fresh thinking, new motivation or a different approach. People I've worked with have used creative approaches for a number of very specific purposes including: better time management, re-engaging with a long-term partner, improving their writing and production skills, self-confidence, team-building, understanding dreams, and many more issues and projects.

So, in summary, there are three possible reasons you may have for working on your creativity:

- to see things in a new way, stepping out of dead-end thinking;
- because you feel you've lost a creative drive that you once had;
- to work on a specific project or issue.

Off the page

Dotted throughout the text are 'Off the page' suggestions. These are practical, creative activities that are designed to help you reflect on the text or to apply it to your situation. If you prefer to read the book without breaking off, you can simply ignore these sections or perhaps come back to them later. A couple are placed on the next page, just to get you going.

Off the page

What are your preconceptions of the word 'creative'?
Write the word in the middle of a sheet of paper and jot
your reactions down around it. What does this tell you
about your attitude? Do you think of creativity as something 'we don't talk about'?

When you've reflected, do the exercise again, but this
time write down words that reflect how you'd like to
think of creativity – chuck out any unhealthy or negative
baggage.

Alternative: Use pictures cut from newspapers and
magazines instead of words.

Off the page

To help you think about why you want to work on
creativity, get into the habit of reflecting on the day,
perhaps just before you go to sleep. Where have you used
your creativity during the day? Where would you have
liked to have been more creative? One way of structuring
this is to look for three examples of using your creativity
and three of where you'd like to have been more creative.

Thought starters

As an alternative way of working with the book, at the close of
each chapter are a number of quotes pulled from the text.
These are meant to be more than a reminder of key points;
indeed some of them are extracted from rather minor points.

The idea is that any one of them might set you thinking in a new direction; perhaps they'll remind you of their context in the chapter, or perhaps they'll take you off to pastures new. If you don't mind defacing the book (and *I* don't mind if you don't), you could make your own set of thought starters by highlighting anything in the text you want to think about further.

The path of wholeness

Chapter 5 gives suggestions for how you might nurture creativity through adopting a discipline leading to wholeness – that is, to a more balanced and fulfilling life, one where you feel more 'you'. It suggests ways that you can use ideas from the book and beyond to meet specific creative targets in knowing yourself, going beyond yourself, learning to live with others and practising creative living.

Look at me, I'm so-o-o creative!

Perhaps this would be a good time to get out of the way the notion that to say we are creative is in some way arrogant or only applies to people who call themselves 'creative'. My take is that we are all creative, that we can't help it, and that even before we consciously think about anything our minds are busy creating. Here's an example:

Recently I was on a tube train, reading a book, when the lights flashed on and off momentarily as they often do as the train rattles along. As the lights blinked I looked down at my book and saw a maggot crawling up the very edge of the right-hand page. I looked again as the lights came back steadily, and realized that it was simply a tiny fold or bend, like a thumb-nail imprint in the edge of the page. The change in lighting and the effect of the lights outside the train as we moved had given a striped look and a sense of movement, and this had all been put together briefly in my mind to represent a maggot. The whole thing was over in an instant but there was one other element that, on reflection, I could see had led to this mental picture. The book I was reading was *The Magus* by John Fowles. 'Magus' is pronounced 'Magg-us', like 'maggot'.

There were several ingredients that my mind worked with: the bent page, the lighting, the movement and the knowledge that I was reading *The Magus*. My mind put all these together to create that illusory interpretation of what I was seeing. Perhaps we can make a first tentative stab at defining creativity by saying that it is the creative mind adding two and two and making an opera, a drawing, a thought, some words, a flower garden, Concorde and concord . . . to name but a few.

So this book is not about learning to be creative; it's about learning to work with your creativity.

Think practical

We tend to associate creativity with grand schemes and geniuses but small, simple, practical ideas for ordinary people are much closer to our everyday experience. You may stumble across some ideas by accident and it's only later that you see their creative potential. For example, during the writing of this book I changed my method of keeping my diary and addresses from paper (separate diary and address book), to a Palm device

– an electronic organizer or Personal Digital Assistant (if ever creativity were needed it's in the area of computer jargon). The device uses a handwriting recognition system that you have to learn for inputting text. I enjoyed getting to grips with this and I started taking notes for this book whenever an idea occurred to me when I was on the train or tube. So this changed how I wrote the book but it also made me think in a different way. If I'm sitting at my computer I tap away merrily getting an idea down, revising it, scrapping it and starting again. That's not so easy when you're writing with a stylus, using an unfamiliar alphabet while riding a bumpy tube train so I was forced to get the essence of my thoughts down in a new way – the essentials only, and in a style that would make sense hours or days later when I uploaded the notes to my PC. Here's what I wrote about this very idea on a tube on my way to a studio in Shepherds Bush; this is just as it came off the Palm with spelling mistakes, abbreviations and all:

> Writing ideas on a different input device such as p pilot or writ with your other hand. Difficulty help to keep thghts short to the point. mobile text msg, post it notes

I think that's pretty self-explanatory – the idea of using a different way of writing your ideas down to force you to think more concisely whether it be on a PDA, text message, post-it notes or even forcing yourself to write with your 'other' hand. It's a small idea, but it made a difference to how I worked as I wrote this book. It is one of the themes of this book that it's better to work on taking small creative steps rather than trying to achieve imaginative leaps forward all the time. Thinking of creativity in this way makes it less intimidating, more appropriate for our everyday lives.

Off the page

Just as writing our ideas in a different way can change how we think, are there things that you do regularly that you could change? Take an alternative route or a different method of transport; or listen to some music instead of watching television? Try reading some poetry if that's not what you usually do, or read a book by an author new to you or from a completely different genre to your usual.

In other words, make the effort to do things differently and see what effect this has on your creativity.

Being creative – there's no escape!

Let's start this section with a thought experiment. Imagine a tub of some fantastic new flavour of ice cream. The tub lid is open, a spoon descends and dips into the rich, tasty-looking surface. It scoops out a generous portion, lifts it and drops it in the bin.

Now imagine exactly the same situation, the same delicious ice cream but this time the spoon lifts it to your mouth, you eat it and it tastes yummy.

What makes the difference between these two versions of the same event? As you think back to the ice cream incident the most memorable thing for you is something that does not exist outside of you – the delicious taste that you experienced. The most important part of the remembered event for you could not have been recorded by any camera, aroma detector or any other measuring device. There are machines that can tell you with great accuracy how creamy, chocolaty, sweet or bitter the ice cream is, but none of them can actually taste it. It seems that there is no objective reality to the most significant part of the experience. The taste experience only exists within minds. You could describe the chemicals and reactions involved; you could measure the nerve activity but the taste . . . that is for you alone. The bin doesn't experience it (though I admit I can't prove that), but you did, your body/mind/brain made a particular sensation – a creative act.

This takes a bit of thinking about because we are so used to thinking that ice cream has a taste. It doesn't. It has a collection of chemicals that interact with our electrochemical systems to transmit information to our brains but in order for this 'qualia', to use the technical term, to be experienced it must be created in the human mind. Creative events like this are woven into the very socks of our reality, but unlike socks you can't take them off. In fact we are creative all the time, our minds constantly making the world afresh from the stimuli that we receive.

The important point that I want us to take away from this thought experiment is that consciousness is, of itself, creative. To be aware of being is to be creative. All of the experiences of the senses are created within our minds, our conscious existence: colour, light, smell, all of it.

From the brain, and the brain alone, arise our pleasures, joys, laughter and jests, as well as our sorrow, pain, grief, and tears . . .

Hippocrates

Creativity and origins

Creativity seems to be built into the system. This is true whether you look at it from a humanist perspective, whether you believe that we are created by God (or gods) or whether you just don't know. In the first case it seems that there is something creative built into the blind process of evolution or that, looking back on this process, it fits our perceptions of a creative procedure (which is another way of saying that we think creatively). The juggling with genes that produces mutation and the ability to adapt and respond to environment can be described as creative.

The Christian tradition in which I grew up begins its holy book by borrowing the Jewish scriptures: 'In the beginning God created . . .' There's enough there to keep you thinking and speculating creatively for a while. How was there a beginning? Is God out of time? How would that work? Can you imagine it? Wiser and more knowledgeable heads than mine have pondered these words but I simply want to draw out the obvious but often overlooked message: Creativity is built in from the word go.

Off the page

Depending on your faith perspective, spend a few moments in prayer or meditation reflecting on the abundant creativity all around you and within you.

If appropriate see if you can find words to give thanks to the original Creator.

If appropriate write words of meditation on the creativity of the universe.

Religion, of course, can be conservative, anti-creativity and anti-innovation, but that's another story and explains why I prefer to talk about spirituality. But take any major faith and you'll see it shot through with creativity – the creation itself, stories, poems, oral tradition, parables and so on; and all of them have a focus on a creative God or gods. I would say to religious believers of all persuasions you can't get away from it, you are called to be creative, creativity defines your God and it defines your existence.

Creativity is also prevalent in a wide range of non-religious philosophies; in fact the very act of thinking about the big questions is creative no matter what conclusions you come to. Let's take an example from one of the most creatively practical philosophies: stoicism, an ancient way whose insights can be applied effectively today and integrated into any belief system. We tend to think of stoicism in terms of 'grin and bear it' but in fact it is more creative and inventive than that. I won't go fully into the spiritual beliefs of the Stoics but a core belief was that we live in a world of continuous change and there are many things that happen to us that we cannot alter. They understood, however, that we could change our thinking and thus how we react to circumstances. When faced with a difficult situation, Stoics try not to waste time asking 'Why did this happen to me?' or 'Why did God allow this?' Rather they start from the position: 'This is where I am. What can I do about it? And what can I learn from this situation?' One can see the danger of always accepting the way things are and, perhaps, not trying to change things, but there is great value and great creative significance in the idea of starting where you are and imagining your options. Sometimes these will be practical. 'I'm in prison for something I didn't do; what steps can I take to put this right?' and sometimes, often, they will be more to do with adopting a state of mind, 'There's no point getting angry with those who put me here, they're not here to receive my angry outburst. How can I move on from this anger?'

Creative metaphors

When we try to make sense of complex or 'mind blowing' questions such as, 'Why are we here?', 'What is conscious-ness?', 'Is my mind "me"?' and the like, we often run up against the limits of our own understanding. I believe that creativity, often expressed through the arts, comes to our aid in these situations. In the Christian tradition, the idea of the Trinity would be a good example of this – it's an attempt to embody beliefs about God that cannot be fully grasped or expressed in 'plain language'. In religious terms it's a mystery. It embodies ideas of three distinct forms that are not only linked but are 'one' while being separate. It is not fully grasp-able or explicable but this is its strength. It is an idea in which we swim. We can inhabit it and explore it, and it resonates with us because it is so like our own experience. We are each many yet one, our families are many yet one and the human race is many yet one, creation is many yet one. It is a powerful and meaningful idea precisely because it cannot be pinned down and 'explained'.

When thinking about ourselves, it is perhaps the mystery of human consciousness that most requires us to use creative metaphors. Currently, many of the metaphors used refer to the mind and brain as like computers, so we talk of things being 'hard-wired', or 'the software of the brain', etc. These terms are fine as long as we recognize that they are simply metaphors born of the computer age, just as the idea of 'humours' is a metaphor of earlier ages. Consciousness resists our attempts to define it and I have a feeling that it is not surprising that we find ourselves in this state, for when thinking about conscious-ness aren't we in the position of Hamlet thinking about Shakespeare? For our consciousness to understand itself, don't we need to turn to other ways of thinking? Do we need to apply this kind of thinking to our spirituality? Metaphor, humour and art are the creative ways forward here because they are able to work with the inexpressible and use words, sound, objects, colour and more to approach what cannot be grasped by our desire to explain.

Off the page
Draw a picture of yourself, not of how you look but of how you feel. In this picture you might have a very large head stuffed full of thoughts and vibrant colours of emotions sweeping through your body or an uncomfortable sensation might make part of your physical body more dominant.

Creativity – the prize

Fortunately we don't have to struggle with these issues in order to make progress because one thing that is self-evident is that creativity is its own reward. As I'm writing this book I'm not actually thinking about its publication or any money that I may earn. I do think about those things at other times (and of course I'm thinking about them now as I write about them – the consciousness question again!) but, generally, while I'm writing, I'm concentrating on writing and there is real joy and a sense of fulfilment in this just as there is when thinking creatively about issues, working on dreams and so on. As I write later, there is a particular creative 'buzz' when working with other people. I accept, and know only too well from experience, that where creativity is concerned there are all sorts of attendant issues such as egomania, arguments about money, who gets top billing and so on; but the actual creative act is its own reward and this is something that tells me that we are made to be creative. This does not mean that if we don't find solutions to our problems we are creative failures, neither does it mean than creativity is the same as originality. The child who mixes paints to make a brown splodgy mess is not being original but she is being creative. So creativity is not solution or explanation or originality but, just like making love, caring for our children, eating and drinking, creativity is natural to us. It nourishes us and it needs no other *raison d'être*.

Off the page

Think about the areas of your life that are their own reward, things that need no other justification; they are simply uplifting, fun, fulfilling, 'feel right'.

Make a decision to seek out those areas and to make space to enjoy them.

Supporting creativity

Before moving on to explore how we can use creativity in our daily lives in the following chapters, I want to mention a few points that I believe are important and that don't have a natural home elsewhere in this book.

Diet

This is not a suggestion or imperative but I do believe that what we eat and drink can have an impact on our creativity. Sluggish minds – think of a boa digesting an antelope – are not likely to be the most creative and we know that there is a correlation between food intake and mental activity. Some people drink a lot of caffeine in a day and describe feeling 'wired'; others feel that they get great insight after a period of fasting. Someone else only has to drink a glass of cola to get 'hypo' and in no fit state for anything that requires relaxed thought. It's beyond the scope of this book to give dietary suggestions or recipes but I do want to plant the thought that thinking about what you take in might affect what you give out – creatively speaking as well as in gastric terms. If you've got a big creative project coming up, or you just want to get into shape for more imaginative work, you might like to think about a detox, a short period of eating and drinking the 'right' things. There are a number of books that can help you do this with recipes and advice.

Humour

I want to add a word about humour because all this talk of creativity can become a little pompous if we allow ourselves to take it all too seriously. I think humour is one of the greatest creative gifts and there's little else left to say, as many a dreary essay on 'what makes me laugh' has revealed. So all I'll say is that, like creativity itself, humour is one of those precious things that is its own reward and I'd urge you, whatever else you do with this book, to have fun.

When things go wrong

I was prompted to add something about this because while I was working on this book, someone I know and love was in intensive care for five weeks and was not expected to live. In fact she did pull through and, as I write, is slowly on the road to recovery but it was a very stressful time and it made me question how creative approaches could be applied when we're facing difficult times. The first thing to say is that there are times when nothing is any use. I've been with people who, at times of real tragedy, have simply fallen apart for a while and it would seem impertinent to offer 'creative solutions'. They don't need solutions; they just need to endure for a while the suffering of grief, the pain of incomprehension, the anguish of losing, or the fear of losing, their world. But there comes a time when creativity can make a difference. I found during those five weeks that things became quite 'stripped down', that, in a strange way, I could see more clearly. Crises can force us to live 'in the now' and there's a sense in which they can help us to see what's really important, putting things into perspective. This, at least, has been my experience but this is a subjective area and your understanding might be quite different. Certainly I found that my creativity wasn't entirely dormant during my many hours spent in the intensive care ward.

Soon after that period I was happily adapting Children's Laureate Michael Morpurgo's book *The Sleeping Sword* for radio. I needed a way to get from one dramatic scene, a diving accident, into the next scene in a hospital. It was the by now familiar sound of the ventilator keeping the patient breathing that came to my rescue. I segued between the sigh of one of the watchers after the accident into that gentle regular mechanical air sound – it does seem that our minds can work on many different levels at once, even when we're facing difficult times.

The exception that I have found to this 'clearer-sighted' view are those times when we become mentally agitated, confused, perhaps depressed and unable to focus our thoughts. In these situations, prayer and/or meditation can play a major part in helping us feel more grounded and better able to cope.

A dash of stoicism can be effective when things are not going well, helping us to accept the situation and to think about where we can go from here. Whatever bad or difficult situations we find ourselves in, climbing out or moving on seems to start with imagining that tomorrow, next week, one day, things will be different; and it is imagination, that inventive reaching into the future, that is our creative first step towards change.

THOUGHT STARTERS

'Thought starters' – the idea is that any one of them might set you thinking in a new direction.

You might find it useful to have a notebook to jot down any ideas that come to you while trying some of the exercises in this book.

We are all creative, we can't help it.

Even before we consciously think about anything our minds are busy creating.

Get creativity out of its box marked 'embarrassing'.

Perhaps you used to have a creative outlet and you've let it drop.

Creative acts are woven into the very socks of our reality, but unlike socks you can't take them off.

To be aware of being is to be creative.

In the beginning God created . . .

Creativity is built in from the word go.

Metaphor, humour and art are the creative ways forward when dealing with big unsolvable questions.

Creativity is its own reward.

Creativity is natural to us, it nourishes us and it needs no other *raison d'être*.

Tragedy or other crises can force us to live 'in the now'.

It is imagination, that inventive reaching into the future, that is our first step towards change.

Whatever else you do with this book, have fun.

2 ✧

The creative path of exploration – dreams, memories and fresh thinking

Don't worry if this sounds more like the title of a whole book than a single chapter! What I hope to achieve here is simply to suggest some different ways of integrating creativity into daily life. The necessary caveats first: this will be idiosyncratic and you will need to work creatively on the ideas here to make them yours; also you will need to fit the suggestions into your own life and I recognize that not everyone has the flexibility to do this easily. I know that on reading these ideas it can seem as though you would need to devote hours of inner reflection and hours more on creative endeavour to get anything out of them. This is not the case; you can achieve a great deal in a few stolen minutes. Perhaps you have a regular train journey or a walk to work or school to pick up the kids – give just ten minutes to creative thought and you might be surprised at how far you can get. You can run thought experiments or find time for musing almost anywhere: in the bath or shower, doing housework, or in bed, for example.

Working creatively with dreams

We'll begin this part of our creative pathway with a spot of sewing. The sewing machine was invented by an American – Elias Howe, born in Spencer, Massachusetts, on 9 July 1819. Or was it invented by the much better known Isaac Singer? As with many technological developments such as radio and television, there are competing claims but we can say with

Off the page

Put some creative thinking time in your diary. Try to identify odd moments, ten minutes will do, when you'll think about what you want to achieve creatively and/or try out some of the ideas in this book.

Be creative about when you'll do this, last thing at night, while travelling, walking the dog . . .

Also, devise and use a secret symbol that you can put in your diary, something that only you recognize and that says 'creative time' to you. If you want to keep it really secret you could disguise the symbol and have an alternative explanation available. That way you get the fun of some gentle subterfuge thrown in for free (though it's not hard to see how this could lead to complications!).

certainty that Elias Howe played a major part in the development of the sewing machine as used today. Howe patented his invention on 10 September 1846. There were legal battles with Singer and with another inventor, Allen Wilson, but the three eventually shared their rights and established a joint patent – the Sewing Machine Combination. This is, of course, a creative story in itself, but what particularly interests me is the vital breakthrough that Elias Howe is said to have made because of a dream. There are different versions of this story and I suspect that some have been 'cleaned up' so as not to give credence to Howe's 'Victorian' view of 'savages' and 'cannibals', but they all retain the essential feature of the 'breakthrough'. Let me retell my favourite version in my own words.

The scene

The race is on to develop the first practical sewing machine. Elias Howe feels a tremendous pressure to make the essential breakthrough. He knows that his whole future and enormous riches depend on being the first. He has been working all day, tinkering and thinking, changing and making, but still the thing will not work – the material snags or the needles break. Exhausted, he finally gives in for the night and goes to bed but his mind is still working and, in his dreams, his subconscious speaks to him, shouts at him until he finally hears . . .

The dream

I am running, running for my life. They are after me – a gang of savages is chasing me and I cannot escape. I run, but know that it is hopeless. I am both running and not running. I am trying so hard to get away but I cannot, and I know that I cannot; and now I know something worse . . . I smell fire . . . I see fire . . . I am to be boiled alive. I am being chased by cannibals!

Now I am in the hot water and it is getting very warm.

Now I am in the very hot water . . . I am burning, boiling, I will die.

I climb out of the pot but the savages, moving as one, lean over and their pointed wooden spears push me back in with a jabbing action.

Again I try to climb out and again I am pushed back – their spears pushing down then pulling back . . . Again I attempt to climb out; again the spears push down and withdraw . . .

I cannot escape, I will die a horrible death, boiled alive . . .

I sit up in bed – it is over. My heart is racing but I say again and again to myself, 'It was a dream, Elias, it was a dream.' The fear is mixed with a joyous relief, an escape – thank God. And then, hot and wet from the horrors of the cooking pot, it strikes me – the spears strike me, but what a happy attack this is; a sharp, pointed, acute and undeniable moment of realization. I see the spears afresh and I realize that their movement is like the needle of my prototype, jabbing down and up; but I also see a detail – every spear has a hole in the sharp end. It is the break-through I have been looking for.

It was indeed the vital breakthrough. All previous attempts had been based on a needle like that used for hand-sewing, with the eye hole at the far end. Howe realized very quickly that he could devise a mechanism that would allow the thread to be poked through the material by a needle with an eyehole at the sharp end, then anchored by thread from underneath, and so the sewing machine was born.

I should point out that some versions of the story do not include the cooking pot – just the 'savages' with their pointed wooden spears – but if the cooking pot were part of the dream it would make sense since Howe's subconscious would be screaming at him that he is in 'hot water' over this problem. Either way, this remains a powerful story of the ability of our dreams to speak to us or, to put it in another way, of the creative possibilities if we listen to our dreams. This is the area I want to explore first in this chapter – working creatively with our dreams.

All my life I have been a thinker about night-time dreaming (and often a daydreamer too but that's another story, one you'll find at the end of this chapter). At one time I took my dreams literally and felt that they were foretelling the future, and indeed I do remember some significant dreams that seem to do this. Then a few years back I read a book that became influential in how I worked with my dreams. The book was *Dream Thinking*, by Alex T. Quenk and Naomi L. Quenk (1995, Davies-Black Publishing). It helped me to explore what my subconscious might be saying to me through dreams, giving an outline of Jung's and Freud's approaches and exploring symbols and puns in dreams. What the book gave me most, however, was a push in the direction of *using* my dreams. I realized that there is no right or wrong here, a dream means something to you if it means something to you. In other words, supposing you dream of doing some ironing and then you reflect on the dream. It might make you think, 'I've got loads of ironing to do, I must get on with it.' Or it might lead you to the conclusion that you're thinking too much about domestic chores and you need to get out more, 'How dull can I get? I'm even dreaming of laundry!' Again, the dream might lead you to think that you need to let yourself get hot and steamy! The point is that it's what you do with the dream, how you choose to let it speak to you that matters. Often I have an 'ah-ha' moment when thinking through a dream, when everything clicks into place and I believe that I've found the real 'message' of the dream. But the meaning wouldn't arrive unless I worked with the dream, unless I brought my creativity to bear on it. I'm not sure if all this is what Quenk and Quenk wanted me to get out of their book but, in creative fashion, it's what I've made of it.

Off the page
What is your 'theory of dreaming'? Do dreams convey
messages or are they random, meaningless? Do they
come only from within you or can they be 'sent' from
other people, God, the future or the past?
    Complete this sentence for yourself: A dream is . . .

I said earlier that I believed that a dream was some sort of
communication from the subconscious, but I don't want to be
dogmatic about this as many dreams don't seem to carry this
function and there may be other possibilities. I recently read a
thesis by Lisa Cornwell, a theology graduate, who believes that
all dreams come from the personal and sometimes collective
unconscious and that God can use this as a medium to
communicate with us in certain instances because God is the
'ground of our being'. There is also a view that dreams can
predict the future, either by divine or other spiritual interven-
tion or through a more scientific process that is caught up with
the quantum view of how consciousness 'works'.

In his book *The Origin of Dreams* (Human Givens Publishing,
1997), psychologist Joseph Griffin suggests that the only function of dreams is to clear the mind of emotional arousal that has
not been 'discharged' during waking time. So if you had a big
row with a colleague and the whole thing was out in the open,
you wouldn't dream about it; but if you were cross and did
nothing about it you might dream about it to discharge the
emotional 'build up'. I'm not entirely convinced by his argument but it does offer another model of why we dream.

However, I mention his book here because he has a fascinating section about how the mind uses metaphor in dreams

(in order to discharge these emotional arousals), and he suggests that the subconscious mind will grab any useful metaphor it can, perhaps including things that haven't happened yet. He suggests that the quantum nature of consciousness might enable the mind to take images from the future. He gives an interesting example of this. A friend of his dreamed of a house full of lizards and interpreted the dream in a helpful way with the lizards symbolizing something he hadn't dealt with. A few days later the man got up in the middle of the night to find – you guessed it – his house was full of lizards. Perhaps this was an image grabbed from the future or maybe it was coincidence.

I can't go any further with this and I can't say definitively what dreams are or why, in evolutionary or spiritual terms, we dream. What I can write about is how we can work creatively with our own dreams and use them to speak to us, regardless of their origin.

Here's one of my dreams:

I am Alexi Leonov, Russian cosmonaut and slated to be the first man on the moon, if only we can beat the Americans to it. I'm training on the Lunniy Korabl, the Russian lunar lander, and as I arrive for the training session my colleague greets me and says, 'Ah, Alexi, we have a gift for you today. Look, Boris made it especially for you.'

'It' is a spongy carpet painted like the lunar surface for me to practise on. I can feel it bounce beneath my feet but I'm not very happy about it because, although it is beautifully made, it is too small. I have to go right to the corner of the training room, off the carpet, to see the whole of the lunar lander.

'Look,' I say, 'I have to go over here to see the whole thing.'

Now I am actually in space and I must separate one stage of the module from another in flight in order to get away safely after leaving the moon. Desperate music is pounding away like in an action film. The 'works', as in all Russian spacecraft, are all exposed, a mass of pipes and wires, and I can't find the right button to press. There's a countdown going on and very soon I will crash. Then with a roar of the engine and an earth- (moon-?) shattering volume of music, I'm free and I feel tremendous relief.

Great dream, eh? Very 'Apollo 13 meets *Thunderbirds*'! The dream was vivid, in Technicolor and with full cinema-style sound so, as I thought about it, I was aware that the dream was shouting at me, pretty forcefully. In order to understand what this dream was about for me you need to know my circumstances and interests and, in particular, you need to know what was causing me angst at the time that I had the dream. All dreams are special to the dreamer and, in the end, your interpretation – what the dream says to you – is the only thing that matters. No one else will be able to get that 'ah-ha' moment when the whole thing clicks into place, though other people can, of course, help you to think it through and contribute ideas. Actually this dream spoke to me loud and clear with just a little mulling over, and it made a practical difference to my life and that of my family – nothing as rewarding as inventing the sewing machine, however!

First let's address the context of the dream – the Russian lunar programme. This is something that I've had an interest in for a while and just before the dream I'd been looking at some newly published photographs of the interior of the

Lunniy Korabl. It doesn't really matter, but the dream was quite accurate in some respects – Alexi Leonov would have been on the prime crew for the first landing mission and he would have landed alone in a craft with what looks like a messy interior of tubes, wires and gauges. Other details of the dream were less accurate – the 'staging' to leave the moon wouldn't really have happened on the Russian design. These details are not relevant, though, as the Russian space programme just provides the metaphor landscape for the dream.

What was the dream saying to me? For two weeks prior to having this dream I'd been struggling with wireless-networking three home computers so that they could share a broadband Internet connection. If you're not into computers, don't worry – all that matters is that it was something technical and I couldn't get it to work. I tried everything and I learnt quite a bit about the settings needed to get the computers to 'speak' to each other. If you *are* into this sort of thing, I was having problems with the IP addresses of the different computers – they kept resetting themselves so the different machines didn't know where to find each other. The 'ah-ha' moment came when I heard what the dream was saying. Like Alexi Leonov in my dream, I was too close. I couldn't see the whole thing. If I was going to get 'lift-off' on this I had to get away from all the complexity – there were too many variables and I didn't know 'which button to press'. So I undid everything I'd done. I started from scratch with the networking and tried to see the 'whole thing'. I simply reread the instructions and I found a tiny, single sentence that I'd been missing, about making sure that all connected devices were turned on at set-up. I did this and the network has worked, with minor unconnected disconnections, ever since.

So this is an example of being too close to a problem and, deep down, I knew this but it took a dream for me to see it. It's that feeling of knowing it all along, but not realizing that you know it. The working out is very satisfying, though. Here's another dream, and this one took a lot of thinking about before I got my welcome dose of 'ah-ha'.

> I am standing on a stage in a kind of school or college hall, but I know that it's actually in the headquarters of the clothing chain Next. There's a tiny trapdoor in the stage and I open it. Beneath the trapdoor is a tap and I reach down and turn it. End of dream.

I puzzled over this one for several days (on and off of course!). My brother worked in the management of Next at the time, based at their HQ near Leicester, so I guessed that this was something to do with it but, try as I might, I couldn't make the symbols 'fit'. The realization of what this was all about started with a single word – pun. I remembered that dreams sometimes used puns and that the mind is immensely creative and wonderfully silly at times. I'll give you some background context and then this punning dream should slot into place. At the time, several years ago, I was getting my first taste of creative training and development work within the BBC and I was enjoying it. I wanted to branch out and see if I could get work in other organizations, but where to start? The dream simply told me (look out for the puns): The *next stage* is to *tap* into *Next*.

It was so obvious – I had a brother there, they had a training and development programme, maybe they could use me? As a result of this I did get in touch with my brother and he was happy to arrange for me to meet his training people and

I did. That's the end of the story. I never did any work for them – this was my first taste of the realities of freelance consultancy – but it was a useful experience and a valuable reminder that while dreams can speak to us, they are not magic. Dream that you have won the lottery and you might – or you might not; or you might be dreaming about someone called Lotty Ree or Hugh Gwin.

So what should you do with your dreams? I'd like to offer some ideas for working creatively with your dreams and, although I can't cover the whole subject, and I write very much as interested and experienced amateur (are there professional dreamers?), there are plenty of books you could look at to take things further if you become passionate about working with your dreams. There are also resources on the Web, and courses and dream groups, which some people find helpful.

A word of caution: I would avoid anyone who claims to be able to offer a definitive interpretation of your dreams – especially if they've never met you or know nothing about you. I'd also steer clear of books and resources that claim to match dream symbols with specific meanings – 'Dreaming of death means birth' and that kind of thing. These belong to an entirely different understanding of dreams, often more in the magical tradition. In my experience, dreams are more powerful than these 'catch all' solutions suggest, precisely because they are yours, built for you and to be interpreted by you. Besides, half the fun is in the creative working out; what's creative about looking up symbols in a book?

Journal
Keep a journal of your dreams, or at least a note. Many people find it useful to keep a notebook by their bed and jot down the

key features of any dream – setting, 'plot', characters, feelings, events and so on. Some people who say that they never dream find that they begin to remember dreams once they develop the habit of 'journaling'. You can use the journal as part of the creative process. It can include, as well as notes on the dream itself, your emerging understanding of its 'message', doodles and sketches, colours and things that the dream reminds you of. In this way a dream journal becomes a working document, part of the creative process.

Off the page

Decorate the cover of your dream journal. Start with a plain cover and then add images or symbolic representations of the dreams within as you write about them. You can use this as an aide-memoire of your dream journeys whenever you pick up the book.

Retell

A good way to recall the details and 'feel' of a dream is to retell it in the first person. So instead of saying, 'I had a dream that I was being chased by robots', say 'I am running, running for my life. They are after me – a gang of robots is chasing me and I cannot escape.' You will find that this adds immanence to the dream; you begin to feel as if it is happening again and you can recall many more details. You may also find that this 'putting yourself in the dream' brings the interpretation closer because you will be working on a feeling rather than a language level.

Off the page
Try writing the dream in the first person in your journal.
  Other ways of retelling the dream:

- As a comic strip with simple pictures and captions;
- As a single illustration;
- As a poem – start by writing down the most significant events, people, symbols and feelings.

Revisit

Once you have found a way to capture the dream, allow yourself to revisit it during the hours and days ahead. Whenever you have a moment, go back over the dream, retelling it using the technique above, until you reach your 'ah-ha' moment and the dream 'clicks'. If it never clicks, don't worry because, if it's something important and you keep listening and reflecting, your subconscious will find a way to get the message through. Alternatively it may be that the moment has passed and the dream is no longer significant for you.

Question

In order to find what the dream is saying to you, ask yourself questions about the dream and about events in your life. Key questions might include:

- What images or symbols are in this dream?
- What seem to be the most important symbols?
- What are the feelings in this dream?
- Could any of the people, events, or symbols be puns?
- What are the big issues in your life at the moment? Might the dream relate to these?

Off the page

Keep track of the big issues in your life. Make a mental note about what you think or worry about most during each day. Look at your dreams as a whole. What are the big themes that emerge? Do these relate to your 'worry list'?

Using your dreams and thoughts, spend a few moments each day (it might be in bed at night) thinking through those concerning issues and, if appropriate, reprioritize them. Ask yourself if they really deserve the amount of attention you're giving them. See if your altered thinking is reflected in your dreams.

Continue

We tend to treat dreams with reverence, perhaps even awe. This is not surprising if you think about it: you go to sleep and you go somewhere else, somewhere where the rules are different and you find yourself in strange and unexpected stories and events. You can fall in love, you can suffer grief and pain, and you can laugh, you can shake hands with a singing tree ... Dreams seem to come to us from 'somewhere else', perhaps deep inside us, perhaps deep inside the universe or the mind of God, so it is probably quite proper that we treat them with respect and 'handle with care'. But they are ours to use and one way to use dreams creatively is to continue them. Think about what would happen next if the dream continued. This can be particularly powerful if the dream has left you feeling unsatisfied, perhaps because you woke up part-way through. It can also be useful if you don't like what the dream is telling you and want to change it.

A good example of this is a colleague who dreamed that she was on one side of a glass wall doing boring paperwork while all her fellows were the other side having a fantastic party. It wasn't hard for her to work out that she felt that everyone else was having more fun and that she felt dull and uncreative compared to her colleagues. Working on the dream, she decided to continue it by opening a door, leaving her drab space and joining the party! This was what she wanted to do in real life so she used the dream to tell this positive story about herself.

Use

In my creativity workshops I use the idea of dreams to help people focus on their own creativity. I ask them, often in pairs, to make up a dream that they can tell to the rest of the group – a dream that they would have if they were dreaming about their own creativity. It's a marvellous way of focusing on what's important, on the essence of the issue. You can use the idea of dreams as a way of exploring any issue: 'I can't get this script right – if I were dreaming about it, what would my dream be?' This process can often highlight and bring to the surface the underlying causes of problems and suggest solutions because, as in dreams, the issues can be isolated, clarified and writ large – often very large as with the colleague who dreamt of a brick wall stretching up into the sky between her and her goals; her solution was to grow bigger than the wall and step over it.

Off the page

Identify an issue or problem that you would like to think through creatively.

Now tell yourself a story. The story starts: Last night I dreamed about (issue or problem) . . .

Continue in your own way. Have fun. Remember that in dreams things and people can take on new qualities (an annoying colleague can be a giant chattering set of teeth for example). How would your creative dreaming mind present the problem or issue to you? Once the imaginary dream is over, go back over it and see what it might be saying to you – what are you saying to yourself?

Before leaving dreams – a perilous thought

Everything I have written about dreams presupposes that dreams are in some way given to us to serve our needs in our waking world – but what if it were the other way round? What if we live to dream and all our experiences while awake are food for our dreaming selves? This is a perilous thought because if it took hold we would not know which reality we lived in or if there is any reality for us to live in at all. I love to dream, but I don't live to dream. However, there is one sense in which I think this 'topsy-turvy' thought might carry some truth. Have you ever had a 'lost chord' experience where something you have dreamt or thought simply won't go into words? Isn't it possible that in the depths of the universe and the mystery of being there are things that our minds cannot grasp, that we can't capture with language? And isn't it also possible that we can touch these realities only in our dreams?

Work with your memories

What's your earliest memory? It's most likely to be something that you've thought about often because this is not an uncommon question to ask. I want to begin this section with some exercises. I suggest reading through the outline below first and then, in a quiet space, taking some time to relax. Once you are relaxed and able to give your attention to your memories, use the suggestions below to help you explore them. Note that you will find more about relaxing and entering the 'altered state' in Chapter 3, so you may choose to return to these exercises once you have read that section.

First, go back, in your imagination, to that earliest memory or to another memory that seems significant to you. Allow yourself time to explore the memory, dwell on it, replay it several times – inhabit it. Some methods for achieving this include:

- Hearing the memory – imagine that you only have its soundtrack;
- Seeing the memory – just the pictures, no sounds;
- Reliving the memory – tell it as if it's happening now;
- Thought-tracking the memory – disregard everything else and concentrate solely on what you were thinking;
- Feel the memory – replay the memory concentrating on the emotions involved.

Each of the above will give you a different perspective on the memory. I want to talk in a little more detail about another 'perspective' approach – point of view. The essential idea is pretty much self-explanatory; you simply replay the memory, each time looking at it from a different point of view.

Supposing you have a memory of your first day at school. Perhaps you remember feeling lost and uncertain, maybe you were given a pencil by the teacher and lost it and this made you feel anxious. Using the point of view (POV) technique, first take your 'master shot'. In filming, a master shot is a view that covers all the action to which all the other shots – the close-ups, tracking shots, pans and so on – are matched. Your own master shot isn't quite like that because it is essentially the 'memory shot'; that is: what you actually remember and how you remember it. It's the memory story just as you've played it out in your head many times before.

Now allow yourself to find some other POVs. A good one to start would be a traditional filmic master shot – one that takes in all the action in one go perhaps from a 'full on' camera position, or from high up looking down. Then you could try picking one of the other people in the scene and seeing the memory from their perspective. In our example of remember-ing your first day at school, if you were to choose the teacher you might find that she hardly notices you and your worry over the lost pencil. It seems a drama of gigantic proportions to you; to her it is next to nothing. You could choose multiple POVs – the pencil, another child, someone looking into the school from outside, an airborne shot . . . The POV technique can be a powerful way of exploring your memory. One of the things it does is to literally give you perspective.

To take the 'starting school' example again: the teacher's perspective gives a very clear indication that this memory is not in fact as traumatic as you thought. In the scheme of things, losing a pencil is not an earth-shattering event. In this case, looking back on the event as an adult, this will hardly be a revelation but with other memories the use of perspective can be more revealing. The following is based on a real memory explored in this way at one of my workshops, used with the permission of the person concerned.

Tea set

When I was about five, I really wanted a toy tea set. I was fascinated by the idea that you could have a tiny teapot and that it would really hold and pour water into the little cups. My mother eventually bought me a plastic tea set and I remember playing with it. The memory is of me arranging the red and yellow cups and saucers with great concentration and precision, then carefully filling the teapot with tap water and pouring out the tea. All this was happening as I sat at the dining room table. Suddenly my concentration was broken when I felt that my brother was watching me. I looked up and saw him smirking. Even at that age, I knew instantly that he was making fun of me, a boy, playing a 'girlish' game with a tea set. The memory has always stuck with me as an early recognition of not fitting the standard roles expected of a boy, and it is something that has worried me quite a bit in relation to my family.

When I explored this memory using the perspective exercise, I began to see it in a different light. First I realized that I couldn't be certain that my brother was smirking at me or, if he was, perhaps it was only an incident, a moment. I saw my parents in the picture and realized that they didn't think I was behaving inappropriately; after all, my mother had bought me the toy in the first place. Finally, I simply gained some perspective. I saw that this was one small incident. Taking a wide angle I felt all the love and support and fun in our family, and realized that I had this memory out of context. I had given it too much prominence.

Off the page

Keep a memory journal – perhaps a small book that you
carry around with you. Whenever you have a significant
memory (as opposed to remembering that you have to
buy some batteries, for example), jot it down. You can
either write the whole memory or, if it's something that
you're familiar with, you could just write a title like
'First day at school' or 'Incident on the roundabout'.

Whenever you find yourself thinking about the same
event again put a tick next to the relevant journal entry.
You could also add more detail at this time if you've
remembered new things – perhaps dating the new entry.

When you have several entries and ticks, look back
over your journal and ask yourself, 'Why am I remembering this? Why is it so significant?' You may know
why immediately but in other cases you might find out
something new about your past and your present.

Bigger perspectives

In the list of possible POVs above I mentioned using an
airborne perspective. I want to expand that by talking about
perhaps the ultimate perspective – the Earth seen from space.
A number of the 27 Apollo astronauts who have travelled to
the moon have spoken of the power of looking back at the
Earth, of the realization that everything you know is 'down
there' in that small, blue-green marble – the only spot of
colour in the darkness. They mention how the whole thing –
families, friends, history, continents, art, evolution . . . everything they have ever known – can be covered by a thumb held
up against the window. That's perspective! You could add that

into your memory POV shot list. Imagine zooming out from your memory, up through the ceiling (if it's an inside job), through the clouds and away into space until the whole world, everything you have known, is a distant floating sphere.

Some Apollo astronauts have also described a moment of realization when looking back at the Earth, something easy to say but difficult to grasp: there really is no up and down. We are so used to the concept of ground below and sky above that it has infiltrated our world view, our religions, our everyday speech: 'She's going up in the world', 'He ascended into heaven', 'the stars above', 'sinking into despair' – there are numerous examples. It takes a real 'ah-ha' moment to make us realize that up and down are only constructs; they are, at best, local conditions. The stars are not 'up there' but all around us. The planets orbit the sun in more or less the same plane, but planets orbiting other stars have their own plane in which they align, and other galaxies are at all sorts of angles to our own. The world isn't flat and neither is the universe; we truly live in a theatre in the round. Build that perspective into your memory. See each event as something that happened in a particular place on a planet that was in a different part of space then (which incidentally is something that always worries me about time travel stories – if I went back in time to this very spot 100 years ago, the Earth might not be there, it might be somewhere else!). All of this can have the effect of seeing your memory in a new context, one in which the memory is still real but it has its rightful place in relation to the rest of your life and the life of the universe.

Distressing memories

I want to say something about distressing memories because some people have things in their past that they either can't think about or which cause them pain to recall. The first thing to say here is that these may well be beyond the scope of this book and you may feel that one-to-one professional help through counselling or psychiatry is needed; or you may find a group therapy session is the answer for you. There is also the fraught question of false memory, which is again way beyond the scope of my knowledge or experience (I think, but how would I know?). The exercises that I have suggested can be valuable in themselves if you feel reasonably comfortable with the memories you are working with and, as I will go on to consider next, they can be a good way of reflecting on your life and choices you have to make. If, however, you feel disturbed or distressed by memories, it is probably best not to dwell on them alone but to seek outside help.

Then and now

One useful approach to working with memories is to ask yourself what they tell you about yourself. Here are some questions to reflect on when thinking about memories:

- Why did I remember this incident?
- Would I still react in the same way?
- What would be a contemporary parallel incident? For example, would I feel lost and uncertain starting a new job, just as I did when starting school? What incident would parallel the lost pencil?
- What does this memory tell me about myself?

Try working on the memory using a range of media. If you like writing, try writing it in different styles. Taking the 'tea set' example, you could write it in the first person as it is presented above, or write it as a dry factual account:

A boy asked his mother for a toy tea set. She gave it to him. He became absorbed in a game with the tea set. At one moment he thought his brother was smirking at him for playing a 'girl's game'.

Or write it as a sympathetic account:

A young boy wanted to express himself through a particular harmless game but the social mores of the time wouldn't allow him to. Why shouldn't a boy play at making and pouring tea? How foolish and oppressive to make fun of him. Children like this need our support, not our condemnation.

You could try writing it as poetry, perhaps using a particular form such as haiku. I should point out here that I know true Japanese Haiku verse is much more than a simple 17-syllable structure of five-, seven- and five-syllable lines; and I know that Japanese 'syllables' are not the same as those in English, so let's just say 'a haiku-like 17-syllable structure'.

> Two boys in a room
> Boy one pours – concentration
> Two – condemnation?

Or you could try to better Shakespeare's apt words in *Twelfth Night*:

> In nature there's no blemish but the mind;
> None can be called deformed but the unkind.

There are, of course, a whole range of writing and other

artistic responses that you can apply to memories, and these can also be relevant to other things you may be thinking about – reflections, decisions, mysteries. I want to move on to consider a few of these other ways of working creatively on our thoughts and memories.

Frame it!

A frame is simply a way of looking at something in a fresh way. I've already mentioned in the section on dreams that thinking about something as a dream can be a useful way of getting to the essence and 'unpicking' the issue, so let's start this section by thinking a bit more about using dreams as frames. I use this method in my creativity workshops. Recently I ran a number of sessions for BBC Radio Drama. These were one-day 'creative retreats' helping those making radio drama, a highly creative business, to reflect on their work and think about where they might go next. Early on in the day I talked about Elias Howe and other creative dreams and asked delegates to work in pairs to make up a short dream of their own – 'What would you dream if you dreamt about creativity, the blocks and opportunities in your creative life?' The results of this were always fascinating and helped people to focus on the key issues for them, such as being stuck in a creative rut, feeling less creative than their colleagues, or feeling bogged down in the non-creative 'paper work' side of production. We could then prioritize these issues and work on them throughout the day.

So you can think of any issue by framing it as a dream. Just to give you some starting points, here are some issues you might look at in this way but, as ever, the possibilities are endless – you can use imaginary dreams to shine a light on anything you want to think through:

- Decisions about work, relationships, money . . .
- Long-term plans – finding out what's important to you . . .
- Thinking about relationships – 'What's happening here? How can we refresh our relationship?'
- Thinking about yourself – 'What sort of person am I? Who would I like to be?'

Dreams are just one type of 'frame'; here are some others with brief explanations.

Draw

If you mainly work in words, why not try drawing your memory, dream or issue? You could use a free-form approach mainly concentrating on colour and shape, or draw it as:

- A book jacket – what kind of book, aiming at which market and what is the essential message you want to convey?
- A comic book – break your thought down into its component sections and tell the story with verve and concise illustrations.
- A cereal packet – is it a children's fun breakfast with free gift, or a posh muesli or granola? What are the essential ingredients?
- An advert – how would you advertise your memory dream or issue? What are the key points to get across?

Game

This is a very effective team exercise that I use with organizations to help them think about important issues. I do it for real with old board-game counters, cards and boards but it can equally well be a thinking exercise, though then it is less detailed and more of a general thought experiment. The idea is simply to take an issue or bundle of issues – let's say it's the company ethos of 'The Jamboree Theatre Company'. The exercise starts by talking through, in general terms, those things that might constitute the company ethos. You might end up with a list including things such as:

- Innovation in theatre;
- Audience-focused;
- Excellent value for money;
- Wide variety of styles;
- Profitable.

Then, working in groups, the delegates are asked to devise a board game that rewards those qualities. Just as when playing Monopoly you win by applying the principles of capitalism to whatever luck comes your way, so in the 'Game of the Jamboree Company', you stand the best chance of winning if you support the company ethos. A simple way to start to build the game is to think of what might be on the 'chance cards':

- 'You win an innovation award – receive 50 extra audience members';
- 'Your latest production is derided as "stale and repetitive" – go back three spaces';
- 'Ticket price changes put extra bums on seats – receive 100 extra audience points.'

You would then need to devise a game, the playing of which, as far as possible, supported the company ethos. How would you win such a game? What kind of board would it have? What part would chance play? You can see that this can be quite a complicated and absorbing exercise. It is great for team-building because, in each team, everyone needs to work together on a complex and multifaceted creative and fun process. It is also a powerful way of examining the issues, requiring the teams to think through the aims of the game and thus the aims of the organization in some detail. It can work with any issue in any organization and can call on a range of skills and personalities from those with number skills, to drawing, writing and imagination.

There are, of course, an infinite number of frames you can use to help you think about any issue in a new way. Some of the better known include questions such as – 'If you were a colour, animal, car, book . . . which would you be?' You can use frames creatively on your own or when working with others and the possibilities are bounded only by your imagination. Now what kind of fruit are you today? Or are you more likely to think of me as a fruitcake?

Off the page

Use the idea of a frame in a simple, almost literal sense, as something that contains an image and something through which you look.

Borrowing an idea from Buddhism, practise using an imaginary frame to create distance between yourself and any situation. When you're feeling tense, anxious or angry, or you feel like intervening in a situation, first step back and imagine you're viewing it through a frame, perhaps as if it's happening on a television screen. You'll see more objectively and feel more detached. Thus you'll be able to think with greater clarity and react more appropriately.

Daydream

I want to end this chapter by saying a little about daydreaming. In our culture, or certainly in the era that I was brought up in, daydreaming was somewhat frowned upon. A daydreamer was seen as someone who wasn't in touch with reality and didn't 'know their place'; had ideas 'above their station'. It has taken me a long time to get over this negative conditioning. Why shouldn't we dream of a better life, a fairer world or being a different or better person? I think this kind of negative conditioning held me back when I wrestled for quite a time to make the decision to leave my relatively secure and well-pensioned job at the BBC in order to freelance.

As someone with radio, TV, innovation, training and development, and online experience, I was pretty sure I could make it through to retirement and pick up my good BBC pension. But I daydreamed of being my own boss, or being able to write more, do more creative work, follow a more flexible course. It was right for me to take my time about this step because of the possible effect on my family and the need to 'do it properly' and minimize the risks. But it was also right for me to daydream as well. I developed my daydream into something a bit more solid; I built a website extolling all my abilities and what I could offer to potential clients. The point is that this website was actually part of the daydream. I built it as if I were already freelancing, already able to offer these services. For me it was an ideal way to think through what I wanted to do, helping me to flesh out my ideas and, crucially, helping me to believe that it was possible. Making the website helped me to move from 'This can't happen' to 'Maybe . . .'

Off the page

There are many things you can do to help flesh out your daydreams and have some fun with them:

- Design a website (could be on paper if you don't have the computer skills)
- Design a logo
- Write a mission statement
- Write/design a brochure
- Set some goals
- Talk to friends
- Research the market

My daydream required a big lifestyle change and a risk all at once but it needn't be like this. Give yourself permission to daydream, then step back and see if there are any parts of the dream that you could achieve. Set a realistic target and see what you can do to bring your dream to life. Daydreaming is nothing to be ashamed of. It's a good, creative tool and you don't know where it might lead on your creative path. A final thought – change the word 'daydream' to 'vision' in the above – does this make it more acceptable?

THOUGHT STARTERS

Work with your dreams – their metaphors and puns.

Your dreams are yours, built for you and to be interpreted by you.

Keep a journal of your dreams.

Work on a feeling level, rather than on a language level.

Use the idea of dreams as a way of exploring any issue.

Isn't it possible that there are realities we can touch only in our dreams?

What's your earliest memory?

There is no up and down.

One approach to working with memories is to ask yourself what they tell you about yourself.

> In nature there's no blemish but the mind;
> None can be called deformed but the unkind.

A frame is simply a way of looking at something in a fresh way.

Why shouldn't we dream of a better life, a fairer world or being a different or better person?

Give yourself permission to daydream, then step back and see if there are any parts of the dream that you could achieve.

3 ✧

The creative path of spirituality, meditation and prayer

One day God came up to me and said, 'Look, Gordon, I'm really pleased with all this creative work you're doing and I'd like to give you a gift, anything you like – just ask.'

Now it's not often that God makes you this kind of offer, so after a moment's thought (I didn't want to leave it too long because the good things in life have a habit of turning into something else before you know it) I said, 'I'd like an instant transport machine so that any time I want to I can step right out of my office directly onto my favourite beach in Menorca.'

God looked a bit disappointed, saying, 'Well, I didn't expect that. I thought it might be something more creative, Gordon, not so self-indulgent and materialistic. The thing is,' God went on, 'that's a highly technological job and technology is more a human thing – you know? I mean, I could do it, but it would take an awful lot of effort. How about something more holistic, more in my line of work?'

'Okay,' I said, 'fair enough,' being an obliging sort of person where God is concerned. 'How about you explain to me the meaning and purpose of life and the reason for suffering and death?'

And God replied, 'What colour did you want that transport machine?'

Spirituality, meditation and prayer mean different things to different people. One reader might feel that she is in touch with God through meditation; others might believe that they have entered into some kind of inexpressible mystery, another reader might feel that he has simply entered into a different state of consciousness and that there is no 'God stuff' involved. Whatever you think about what I say in this chapter, my hope is that you'll take anything useful and apply it to your own outlook.

For me spirituality is about something that we can't adequately express but which is approached by words such as 'connected', 'whole', 'in touch'. Spirituality is about inspiration, not dogma; it's about things that are unknowable but towards which we reach; it's about personal and shared progress towards wholeness. Behind all this is the idea of exploring our relationship with all creation, of seeking understanding and communion with God. But since God cannot be captured or defined I feel quite comfortable with a notion of spirituality that leaves this open. That is why I wouldn't want any readers to feel that this isn't for them unless they subscribe to a certain set of beliefs. As I suggest earlier, I believe we can approach the reality of existence, faith, God, and what it is to be human only through creative engagement, through music, art or drama for example, and that if we think we've found 'it', we surely haven't for these greater truths cannot be captured and caged.

Another aspect of my understanding of spirituality is that the question 'Is there a God?' is more meaningful than any answer could be. It is the ability to ask abstract questions, to feel and experience the world, to be a conscious entity that is the defining miracle; this is the inexplicable state of human awareness and for me this is God-stuff but also something that we take for granted. We allow ourselves to think that it is normal to think, feel and experience but in fact it is extraordinary – ask any rock, computer or planet. Where spirituality is concerned we are rather like our dog, Pepper, who we take on walks, sometimes driving a few miles to one of a number of country areas. Like Pepper, we're on a journey and we don't know where it will take us (sometimes a nature reserve, sometimes a river, sometimes my parents, two hours' drive away, sometimes the vet's). We don't understand how we are transported. We only know that when we get there we discover good things, good smells or – in the case of the vet – things happen to us that are for the best but don't feel like it at the time. To put this in other words, we don't understand what we don't understand; we are not yet what we will be and our responsibility in the here and now is to continue the journey.

So we should start from where we are and work with what we have – the faith part of spirituality is, for me, the positive, creative use of the here and now. You don't need to have it all worked out before you start working with it; there's no point trying to figure out exactly what you believe if this process stops you functioning.

Creativity is an essential tool in this and I see a clear connection between creativity and faith. In the New Testament, faith is described as 'the assurance of things hoped for, the conviction of things not seen' (Hebrews 11.1, RSV). This phrase can also be applied to any creative endeavour where we are actively engaged in seeking an outcome, such as a work of art, or writing a story. Part of the creative process is faith that there will be an outcome, that we are going somewhere with our creativity. We begin where we are and look towards an end goal that we have not seen. I believe that the same is true for science, invention, arts, relationships, spirituality and all human exploration. The big questions – questions of meaning, purpose and destiny – keep us moving forward in a creative way so explorations of faith and creativity come together again.

Off the page

Look at the pictures or art objects that you have chosen to live with – those that are in your home or that you carry around with you.

Choose one at a time and look at it and perhaps touch it for a few moments. Then carry it with you in your mind throughout the day. Dwell on it whenever you can, asking yourself what memories it evokes, why it is important, how you felt in relation to it when you first acquired it and how you feel about it now.

Gradually, over a period of time, move through the chosen objects in your life. Then ask yourself if anything is missing. What would you like to add? What objects would represent a statement that you want to make about your life now or your hopes for the future?

Seek out pictures and objects to add to your collection. One good way of doing this is always to carry a camera and make your own creative decisions. They don't have to mean anything to anyone else – it's your space (even if you share a living space there should be part of it for you and there's always your wallet or purse) so fill it with your art!

On my office wall I have a photograph of a bluebell wood that I took at a time when I was coming towards some kind of crisis and was facing big decisions that I didn't feel equipped to take. It's quite a good photo but it's not anything particularly original. It doesn't offer much in the way of insight to anyone except me. For me it symbolizes a moment when I was reaching forward, wanting to be different and to make changes. The mind picture that I used of that 'good future' was of standing in the midst of those bluebells – again not an original or clever idea, just something that worked for me at that time. Now I'm living in that future, and I use the picture as a reminder of the steps that I took: how I was then and how I am now. Is this a story of creativity, or of faith? Is it a spiritual story?

Before moving on, let's take stock. What is your understanding of spirituality? Consider each of these statements – which do you agree with? Which speak most tellingly to you? Are there any that you feel you should reject?

- Spirituality is a journey.
- Spirituality is creative.
- Spirituality is about things that are unknowable but towards which we reach.
- Spirituality will not go into words.
- Spirituality starts from recognizing that we are not yet what we shall be.
- Spirituality is a relationship with something bigger than ourselves.
- Spirituality is the search for meaning.
- Spirituality is the search for God.

Off the page
Write your own succinct definition of spirituality; try to make it as short and clear as possible.

How do you manifest your spirituality?

This is another way of thinking about spirituality; asking yourself where and how you see it at work in your own life. This is an open question and I don't want to close it up again by trying to answer it for you, so please ignore my categories if they're not the ones you would choose. But to get you thinking, here are some possible areas for consideration:

- *In your searching and questioning.* Do you have reflective times when you try to make sense of life and ask yourself the big questions about meaning and purpose? Would it be true to say that you sometimes seek God or 'something bigger' or 'higher' than yourself? Is this part of your spirituality?

- *In attempting to express the inexpressible.* Do you try to find ways to 'say' what simple words cannot express, such as feelings of love, of awe or a response to nature or some personal experience? Do you respond through poetry or artwork or daydreaming? Is this part of your spirituality?

- *Through formal religion.* Do you belong to a church or other religious group? If so, are you able to use its resources, teaching and fellowship to explore your own spiritual path in union with others? Is this part of your spirituality?

- *Through private meditation and prayer.* Do you practise times of meditation and/or prayer when you try to get in touch with your own thoughts or link up to something bigger, such as the whole of creation or God? Is this part of your spirituality?

- *Through reading.* Do you have a holy or special book or books that give you inspiration and that help on your spiritual journey? Do you find spiritual inspiration in a range of books? Is this part of your spirituality?

- *Through other people.* Do you have the ability to 'see God in others' or recognize people as your bothers and sisters? Is the shared, communal nature of life part of your spirituality?

- *Through creative acts.* Do you have a sense of the connection between the creative and the spiritual? Do you feel that you are on your spiritual journey when you are engaged in creativity? Is this part of your spirituality?

- *Through listening to your inner calm.* Do you have a sense of affirmation deep within you that tells you that, wherever you are at the moment, however you feel, you are secure or blessed or 'special'? Is this part of your spirituality?

Off the page

Do your own 'spirituality audit'. Think back over the past week and note down any activity, including thinking and daydreaming, that you would consider to be part of your spiritual journeying.

Be honest with yourself. If, for example, you went to church, was that part of your spiritual journey? Did it take you further forward? Ask the same about any books you read that were supposed to be spiritually inspirational. Consider your relationships with other people in this light.

Ask yourself what you need to continue your spiritual journey and start to think about where you will get it.

As I say above, your list may be quite different and not have much overlap with this. I should point out that I am not trying to hijack human activity and bracket it all together as 'spirituality'; you can easily have a strong sense of communality or creativity without needing to see this as 'spiritual', but these are human characteristics that can support our understanding of spirituality.

Creative approaches to meditation

Meditation is thinking about something by entering into an altered state. If that sounds at all scary let me say that we live much of our lives 'not in the present' and that what I call an 'altered state' is perfectly natural and normal. Here are a few examples.

> You go out of the house in the morning, locking the door behind you. When you think back on this, can you actually remember locking the door? Probably not, because your thoughts, at the time, 'were elsewhere'.

> You're driving and listening to a radio play or to some music. You're wrapped up in what you're listening to. Does this make you an unsafe driver or are you able to safely enter the 'altered state' of being engaged with what you're listening to?

> You're eating a sandwich, looking out of a train window, but you're daydreaming about arriving at your destination. You're not living 'in the now', you're 'off somewhere else' in your mind.

You might note that all of the examples I've chosen are about going somewhere. I find meditation easiest when I'm on the move and this also raises the link between travel and our inward journey.

There are various estimates as to how much of our lives we live 'not in the present' and of course the time will vary from person to person. But it seems that we spend much of our awake time in an altered state. We are alive, aware and functioning but not fully engaged with the present. (Some of us are like that a lot of the time, according to our nearest and dearest!)

So meditation – slipping away from the present reality and thinking deeply about something else – is not that different from the way we think a lot of the time anyway. The major difference is that it is planned and purposeful, undertaken with some goal in mind. Before going on I would like to suggest some creative approaches to meditation.

Getting ready to meditate

Many readers will want to skip this section as it will be similar to things you've read elsewhere: location, breathing, relaxing, and drifting down, that sort of thing. I include it for completeness. If you are skipping, see you 'When you've arrived'.

Location

All you need for somewhere to meditate is somewhere you can meditate. In other words it doesn't have to be a special place with special facilities, just somewhere that allows you to meditate. I do most of my meditation on train journeys lasting about 40 minutes, and I use between ten and 20 minutes of this time. This works fine for me on trains that are not usually very crowded and I find that I can easily move in and out of the meditative state if I need to move or show my ticket. You may need a more peaceful setting and, of course, the nature of the space might vary depending on the kind of thinking you want to do. A bus might be fine for a quick ten-minute meditation but you might need a quiet, comfortable, warm and private space for something longer and deeper. The best advice is to try out different locations and see what works for you.

Posture

When you have your space, you need to adopt a comfortable and relaxed posture. This can be anything that fits the criteria for you. If you can and like to lie down, the classic Alexander Technique position is relaxing and good for your body: head supported so that the neck is not bent (two videos are right for me), legs drawn in with knees pointing to the ceiling so that the spine is not arched, palms resting on the stomach so that the arms are comfortable and relaxed. If you're not sure what's right for you there are more detailed suggestions on the Web and in specialist books.

If sitting, aim for a properly supported spine with feet flat on the floor. Really the only considerations for posture are:

- Is it comfortable?
- Is it healthy?
- Can I sustain this position for the time I wish to meditate?

Breathing

Once you're comfortably positioned begin to become aware of your breathing and slowly take deeper and deeper breaths. Enjoy this relaxing time and concentrate on the good feeling of air going into your lungs and out again. Think about getting the air right down deep into your lungs, a little deeper with each breath.

Relaxing

When you are comfortably breathing in a slow, regular and deep fashion, move on to consciously relaxing your body. Start with your toes and work through your whole body to your head. Tense and then relax each set of muscles a couple of times; so tense your toes, then relax them, and repeat this before moving on to the tops of your feet, your calves and so on. When you get to your face, there are lots of muscles to experiment with but you might prefer to skip this bit if you're on public transport.

Whatever you do, breathing and relaxing, try to take joy in it; you'd pay money, if you're a health spa sort of person, for an in-depth relaxation experience, and here you can get it for free, pretty much whenever you want.

Drifting down

Now turn your attention to the mental and imaginative aspects of getting ready to meditate. This will vary from person to person but it does seem that, for most people, some kind of visualization of drifting into a deeper state is useful. This might involve imagining that you are walking down a hill, or flying gently down or parachuting into a favourite spot (I use that beach in Menorca, of course), or descending a long staircase. Some people find it useful to accompany this with a countdown from 100, 50 or 20. You may be one of the small group of people who prefer to imagine that they are ascending into the meditative state. As in so many creative things – try it out and find what works best for you.

When you've arrived

If you're a skipper, welcome back.

Now you're in your relaxed meditative state, what are you going to do there?

You can do whatever you want; you can go anywhere, meet anyone, consider any issue or just drift about in a relaxed fashion and enjoy the peace. Here are some possible ideas, all involving some form of visualization, so a quick word about that first. Visualization involves imagination, thinking about what you might see in a given situation; so you might visualize a favourite place or an imaginary scene. Nature scenes are popular 'settings' for meditation; imagining a warm day in a beautiful natural environment, for example. It's interesting that many people's pictures of heaven involve this sort of imagery, including those who've had near death experiences. Although it points to the visual, visualization includes the other senses: the feel of grass beneath the feet, the heat of the sun, and the smell of the sea, for example. It also includes feelings and emotions. Before we move on to the examples, can I suggest that you treat them merely as ideas to be adapted and shaped to what you want to achieve through meditation.

Meditation: what's about?

Using the above techniques take yourself to somewhere that you can explore, an imaginary or real place, somewhere where you feel comfortable and relaxed; we'll use a beach in this example.

Tell yourself that you're going to look around and see what you can find and that everything you find will tell you something about your life at present. You'll be looking for things that will point to what interests you, concerns or worries you, things that show how you feel about yourself at the moment.

Then start looking around. You can go anywhere; if you want you can breathe underwater and find things on the seabed. You might find caves to explore, meet people, go fishing ... you can go wherever your meditation takes you, and do whatever you feel like. When you find an object, ask yourself what it might be saying about you and to you. Don't worry if you get stuck or the meaning 'won't come', just enjoy the feel, colour or shape of the object. A good starting point for thinking about what you find is to ask yourself, 'Why did this catch my eye? Why did I pick it up in the first place?'

When you've found a few things, group them together and look at them again. Before leaving the meditation try to sum up what your exploration has told you. Here's an example, just to give you the idea.

I found:

- A fish that I followed and caught – I'm looking for something fresh and lively in my life.
- A rock pool that I kept the fish in – I want to keep something (an idea, a project, a hope) alive and nurture it.
- A pile of dirty, smelly litter – there are some things that I need to attend to and clear out.
- A shiny shell, like a mirror – I need to take a good look at myself and assess where I'm going.
- An old, broken necklace – there are relationships that are important to me where I need to do some healing.
- A set of my own footprints in the sand – I'm on a journey and need to move on.

Meditation: I am there

Use this approach to help you to enter into a situation. This could be anything that you want to think about and understand more fully. It could be used to see things from someone else's point of view, in which case you'd imagine the situation from their perspective, following their actions and thoughts. This approach is often suggested in spirituality books when considering Bible passages for example, drawing on the

Off the page

Develop a simple acrostic to help you enter into the meditative state. You could create your own version of BREATHE, which I've given as an example, or make up an acrostic for RELAX (you might need to cheat a bit on the X!), DREAM or CHILL.

> Breathe in and out slowly.
> Relax your muscle groups one by one.
> Enter the meditative state by imagining
> a downward journey . . .
> And
> Then
> Hit the ground softly and
> Explore.

method of St Ignatius of Loyola. So you could imagine that you're in Jerusalem at the time of the passion and resurrection of Jesus, or you're hearing the Sermon on the Mount, or you're in the boat when Jesus stills the storm. Try to picture the scene, concentrating on the details. If you're in the boat, where are you sitting? How does the storm first appear? How do you feel? and so on. You might choose to go over a small part of the story several times, adding more detail each time, or that may not suit your approach if you prefer to get 'stuck in' to the story as quickly as possible. An important aspect of this kind of meditation is to ask the question, 'What does this say to me?' and a way of beginning to answer this is to start by asking why you chose this particular story in the first place. By way of example, let's look at the stilling of the storm story and think through how you might apply it to your own life. You might ask:

- What storms are raging in and around me at the moment?
- Who is in the same boat with me?
- How can I get to a place where I can hear and respond to 'Peace, be still'?

The answer to the last question might be further meditation. If you're a Christian believer you might like to visualize Jesus using the same words to still the storms you face. Try to imagine the scene. How do you see Jesus? Does he have a natural authority, which calms the troubled waters? Can you see the same thing happening for you? Don't feel upset or a failure if this doesn't work for you. It's not magic and it's not about the strength of your belief. It is just another way of exploring your faith and applying it. It may work quickly for you or it may take longer.

You can use the 'I am there' approach for any situation, such as imagining your own future or something you want to achieve. We'll take an example of writing a novel. In this instance, start by imagining yourself having written the novel and choose a celebratory scene, such as going into a bookshop and seeing stacks of your book selling fast, being interviewed on a chat show, receiving a large royalty cheque . . . Enjoy the daydream aspect of this and then, when the time feels right, go back a bit in time, a little nearer to the present day. Picture the different stages you will go through to achieve that final celebratory scene. Work backwards through the story until you get to now. You've meditated on how to achieve your goal through small steps, now come back to the present out of the meditative state (see 'Returning' below, p. 74) and take that first necessary step.

Meditation: lose yourself

One type of meditation practised particularly by Eastern religions is the use of a mantra, repeated words such as the famous 'Hari Krishna, Hari Krishna, Krishna Krishna, Hari Hari . . .' The idea here is to free your mind from everyday concerns by repeating the mantra. The effect can be a kind of hypnotic trance leading to a different sort of awareness. Some find this a freeing experience, one that puts them in touch with a higher reality or a sense of God and of the unity of creation. The best-known Christian version is probably the 'Jesus prayer': repetition of the words, 'Jesus, Lord, Son of God, have mercy on me, a sinner.'

I have some reservations about this form of meditation because I worry about the power of suggestion in repeating the same words over and over again. I wonder if they can bury themselves deeply in our subconscious (which many would say is the idea) and I'm not at all sure that having the idea 'I'm a sinner' at the heart of our being is particularly healthy.

Where I do find meditation of this sort powerful and helpful is when one needs to 'lose oneself' in order to deal with a particular situation. Perhaps you've just had an angry outburst of a type you've been trying to control, or you feel immensely embarrassed about something you've said or done. In these and similar situations it can be good to use meditation to distance yourself from the circumstances, calm down and then reflect on them.

Let's imagine that you've just had an argument with a neighbour and you feel that, yet again, you didn't handle the situation well. You went over the top and said some things you would have been better off not saying. In this kind of situation you may find it hard to relax into the meditative state but if you've practised you should be able to use the simple techniques above to calm down. If not, at least practise deep breathing; this is a great help in relaxing our tensions. Also don't worry if your concerns keep coming to the surface as you're trying to meditate. Just acknowledge them but don't dwell on them. Return to the meditation, repeating any of the above steps that you need to in order to reconnect to the meditative state.

Once you have relaxed sufficiently to begin to meditate, try to see the event with some sort of perspective. See the situation in the round. The immediate feeling will probably be that this loss of control defines you, that you really are that sort of person, but perspective will help you see that although this is a regrettable aspect of your character, it is not all of you. Try to conjure up some simple recent memory, perhaps something earlier that day, which gives the lie to this negative view of yourself. Perhaps you remember putting yourself out for someone or sharing a joke or playing with your children. There's more on perspective and memory in Chapter 2 and you can use ideas from there to help with your visualization.

Next develop a simple, short phrase that you can repeat as you meditate. Here are some suggestions:

- I lost my temper but I don't lose my temper all the time.
- I acted badly but I can work on this.
- I did something that wasn't clever but that doesn't make me worthless.
- I'll put this behind me and move on.
- I'll learn from this and move on.

Say it to yourself a few times as you meditate. It seems that things that we internalize in the meditative state stay with us, so you should find that meditating in this way helps you cope with the situation now and in the future. I like to stay aware of what I'm saying to myself and not allow it to develop into a repeated mantra where I lose the sense of meaning but, as ever, it's a question of trying things and finding what works for you. If it's a persistent problem, spend a few moments every day meditating in this way to help you see things differently and ultimately change your behaviour.

Meditation: chair of the board

This idea for meditation is based on a Jungian approach explored by Steve Shaw in his book *Dancing with Your Shadow* (SPCK, 1995). We'll start by revisiting the above scenario – an argument with your neighbour. Begin by picturing what's going on in your mind as a kind of board meeting. At the head of the table is a chair, which is meant to be occupied by your healthy ego – your positive, whole and balanced sense of self: the chair of the board. Seated around the table are several of your shadows, aspects of your personality that you can't ignore and which are part of you – such as your anger. Your shadows might include:

- Desire to succeed at all costs;
- Feelings of hopelessness;
- Feeling a lack of self-worth;
- Self-pity;
- Arrogance . . . and so on.

Who's in the chair at the start of the meditation? Who's running the meeting? In the case suggested above it might be an angry shadow who's taken over and is suggesting that he is the 'real you'. In the meditation, picture the board meeting and imagine politely but firmly putting the 'angry you' back in its proper place while the healthy balanced ego takes the chair once more. In effect you're saying to your anger that it still has a seat at the table, it's just not in charge. Your angry concerns will be heard (Why did you get angry at your neighbour? What was the spark? To what extent was anger justified?), but they won't be running the show.

You can use this technique at any time. One idea is to go back over the day and think through who was in the chair at various points. How would the situation have changed if the healthy balanced ego had been in the chair?

Off the page

Try meditating while drawing or writing. Go through the breathing and relaxing exercises while comfortably seated with writing and drawing materials to hand or seated in front of your computer. When you reach the meditative state, open your eyes slowly and begin to explore through drawing and/or writing. So in the example above you might sketch the different 'shadows' at the table and/or give them appropriate names. You may find that this takes a bit of getting used to but it is worth persisting because the end result is something tangible that you can think about and refer to later. I wonder if, when we write or draw, we are always doing so in this kind of meditative state . . .

Meditation: decision

If you have a decision to make that is worrying you, use meditation to help you picture possible outcomes of the different choices available to you. This can be powerful because often, when we are anxious, we exaggerate and overplay in our minds the possible outcomes of a course of action. Often the anxiety comes from the fact that we see all possible outcomes as potentially disastrous and we are caught between them, unable to think clearly.

We'll take a new example to explore this. Steve's partner Josie has a job interview. It's a job she very much wants and she stands a good chance of being appointed. Steve has been encouraging but now he's anxious about it because the job would involve a long-distance move for the two of them. He feels that he's being forced to give up his home but he feels that they're well settled and happy where they are. Also running through his head is the thought that there might be a promotion for him in a few months' time and he'd rather stay put for that and then decide what to do. He can see that Josie is very excited about this job possibility and he doesn't want to upset her now.

It is quite likely that, reading this situation objectively, you can see immediately that the one thing this couple must do is talk and that Steve should air his concerns. I suggest, however, that although this seems obvious from the outside, it will look and feel very different to Steve and Josie. Human relationships are messy, confusing, convoluted affairs, like spaghetti in a bowl. Steve and Josie are in the bowl, not looking down from above as we are.

If you're facing a decision like this, you can use meditation to help you imagine possible outcomes and one way of doing this is to use a smiley face/sad face method.

First identify the different decisions you could make. In Steve's case he could decide to keep quiet and go along with things or he could decide to discuss with Josie the fact that he doesn't want to move. There are other things he could decide to do – such as talking to a friend or writing a letter to Josie, for example – but we'll stick with the first two options for now.

Taking each possibility in turn Steve could, through meditation, see first a smiley face outcome, then a sad face outcome, then another smiley face outcome followed by another sad face outcome, and so on.

Taking 'keep quiet and go along with it' as our example:

> Smiley face: Josie doesn't get the job and we
>   carry on as before.
> Sad face: Josie gets the job, we move and I'm
>   unhappy.
> Smiley face: Josie gets the job and it turns out to
>   be a brilliant move for both of us.
> Sad face: Josie accepts the job and I then tell her
>   of my thoughts; she gets angry and we split
>   up . . . and so on.

It's important that the meditation is visual, not just textual as in the suggestions above; you need to enter into the possible futures imaginatively to get the deepest understanding out of this. Following through this kind of meditation can help you to be more objective about a situation and reach a more balanced decision. Let's hope Steve gets the message early on that talking as soon as possible is the only way forward, as it so often is.

Meditation: words, words, words

This is a very simple idea. You take some words into the meditative state with you and consider them in a focused way. Unlike the 'mantra' approach above, the idea is not to repeat the whole phrase but to break it down and get the feel of its meaning by looking at individual words and how they work together. As a visual image, imagine taking freshly baked bread into the meditation; then breaking it open, releasing its freshness, aroma and textures.

Perhaps you are meditating on:

> Our remedies oft in ourselves do lie
> Which we ascribe to heaven.
> *All's Well that Ends Well*

First examine it whole and try putting its essence into your own words. You're not trying to match the poetry (though you could try!), just the meaning:

- We can do things for ourselves; we don't have to rely on providence.
- The answer lies in us.
- We see God acting when there is no need.
- God helps those who help themselves.

Then imagine breaking open the phrase like that freshly baked bread. Take a word such as 'remedies'. Enjoy its shape and 'flavour'. You could ask yourself what kind of images the word conjures up for you. You could ask what 'remedies' you have in your life: medicines perhaps but also stress-busting, holidays, good books, friends and so on.

The idea is to take the key words and enjoy fleshing them out. Once you've done this for all the important words, imagine eating the bread and thus taking the whole phrase into yourself. What does it mean for you now and how might it change you?

Here are some phrases you might like to meditate around in this way:

Shakespeare

> In nature there's no blemish but the mind;
> None can be called deformed but the unkind.
> > *Twelfth Night*

> The course of true love never did run smooth.
> > *A Midsummer Night's Dream*

> I do love thee, and when I love thee not,
> Chaos is come again.
> > *Othello*

> Things sweet to taste
> Prove in digestion sour.
> > *Richard II*

> There are more things in heaven and earth, Horatio,
> Than are dreamt of in your philosophy.
> > *Hamlet*

> The quality of mercy is not strained,
> It droppeth as the gentle rain from heaven.
> > *The Merchant of Venice*

> We are such stuff
> As dreams are made on,
>   and our little life
> Is rounded with a sleep.
> > *The Tempest*

Simply the thing I am
Shall make me live.
All's Well that Ends Well

Taoist philosophy

The earth seeks no reward; only respect.

Patience is gold.

Defeat is the mother of success.

The gods are within us.

We create ourselves.

Prejudice towards others stops us seeing our true selves.

Sayings of Jesus

Whoever is not with me is against me.

Luke 11.23 (NRSV)

Whoever is not against us is for us.

Mark 9.40 (NRSV)

Let him who is without sin among you be the first to throw a stone.

John 8.7 (RSV)

Unless you turn and become like children, you will never enter the kingdom of heaven.

Matthew 18.3 (RSV)

Love your enemies, do good to those who hate you.

> Luke 6.27 (RSV)

I have come that they may have life, and may have it in all its fullness.

> John 10.10 (REV)

Do not store up for yourselves treasure on earth.

> Matthew 6.19 (REV)

Ask, and you will receive; seek, and you will find; knock, and the door will be opened to you.

> Matthew 7.8 (REV)

Have the salt of friendship among yourselves, and live in peace with one another.

> Mark 9.50 (GNB)

Book of Proverbs

Don't be glad when your enemies meet disaster, and don't rejoice when they stumble.

> Proverbs 24.17 (GNB)

An honest answer is a sign of true friendship.

> Proverbs 24.26 (GNB)

The rich and the poor have this in common: the LORD made them both.

> Proverbs 22.2 (GNB)

If you sow the seeds of injustice, disaster will spring up.

> Proverbs 22.8 (GNB)

Riches will do you no good on the day you face death, but honesty can save your life.

Proverbs 11.4 (GNB)

Without wood, a fire goes out; without gossip, quarrelling stops.

Proverbs 26.20 (GNB)

Off the page

Whenever you come across them, jot down interesting sayings that you think are worthy of longer consideration, creating a notebook of meditation ideas.

A larger book can store images – postcards, magazine pictures and the like – that might be stimuli for meditation.

Returning

When it's time to return from the meditative state you'll need to ease the transition back to normal awareness. There are several ways you can do this.

Reverse the countdown process by imagining you are climbing back up the steps or floating into the air, or slowly ascending from the bottom of the ocean, becoming fully aware as you break the surface. You can count up as you go, you'll probably find that you only need a short count up – say to ten.

Gradually become aware of your body again, identifying the same muscle groups as when you moved into the meditative state. Gently flex each set of muscles as you sit or lie to bring them back to life.

You could use a simple ritual of your own devising, using

words alongside your imaginative pictures such as, 'My journey is done and I return to my conscious home.'

After a period of meditation, give yourself time slowly to become fully aware, stretch your muscles and move carefully. Perhaps have a drink of water to refresh you and to enjoy a physical experience after so much imagination.

Creative approaches to prayer

You might feel that this section is not for you if you're convinced that the line is down and the house is empty at the other end; but you may feel, in the true spirit of the creative individual, that it might contain insights you can ponder and new ways of thinking you can consider.

Much of what I've written above about meditation also applies to prayer. Certainly the suggestions concerning breathing and relaxing, but also those about using some kind of ritual to clear your mind of everyday clutter, helping you to focus on what you're praying and who you're praying to. This may be problematic if you find it difficult to picture or imagine 'who you're praying to' but I have found that you can work creatively with your uncertainties, finding new ways in and new ways of understanding, and that sometimes these lead to a deeper, more honest type of prayer. The important thing is to start where you are and not to be overly concerned with believing the 'right thing in the right way'.

Perhaps I can give an example from my own thoughts. The central act of the Christian story is the death and resurrection of Jesus. I've read and talked endlessly around the idea of redemption and I've found many engaging and thought-provoking ideas, especially around the notion of God's power being made perfect through weakness. But I have to say that I haven't yet been convinced by any particular theory of redemption. I've puzzled over it and argued around it quite a bit but because I believe that you can't choose what you believe, I have to confess that I've not found a version of this theorizing about redemption that I can internalize with the joy that says, 'Yes, I get it.' But if I forget the theology and concentrate on the story, then something powerful happens. I have no problem with the idea of resurrection – it seems such a wonderful end (and beginning) to the narrative. In fact I find the whole notion thrilling, surprising, daring and exciting, and out of this grows something that I guess would be called a belief, something that could be seen as theology. It's simply the idea that no matter what happens, no matter how dreadful things may seem, the light of life, the creative consciousness-making gift of God, cannot be snuffed out. The light shines in the darkness and the darkness cannot overcome it. I find this idea inspirational in the very literal sense that it helps me get through difficult times and informs an optimistic outlook.

All I can say is that the story of the resurrection resonates with me in a way that the theories of redemption do not, giving me hope in the here and now. And when I take this belief into my understanding of drama and literature, and mix it up with the idea of catharsis through tragedy, I think perhaps I do get to some kind of understanding of redemption. Watching the much-loved film *It's a Wonderful Life*, we are taken on a painful journey of broken dreams and loss of hope, into the life of someone who feels his life has been a waste. Then, through masterly story-telling, we experience with James Stewart as George Bailey a joyous resurrection following a period of terrible suffering and self-doubt. This is cathartic; it moves us within the story but we also come out of the film feeling better about ourselves, redeemed by the experience.

That's as close as I can currently get to the idea of redemption. It may not do for you, but for me watching *It's a Wonderful Life* is a most powerful form of prayer.

Off the page

Do you have an image of God? Is this something you can approach through words, painting or other art forms?

What are the elements that make up your idea of God? How did you come by them? How have they changed over the years?

Explore this through meditation.

Prayer: the big picture

Start your time of prayer with an attempt to gain some perspective (for more on this see Chapter 2), stepping aside from your immediate concerns. Here's an approach I use in the form of cheesy, sci-fi, film-trailer voice-over:

> There is a world where no one knows anything.
> The people wonder who they are and what
>   their ultimate destiny is.
> They are alone, cut off from the rest of the galaxy;
>   lost in an unknown universe.
> One woman (man) stands alone,
> Silent before the rushing questions, seeking
>   communion with her universe,
> In a quest for her creator.
>
> Hear her speak . . .

Or you could write a preparation to pray like a book blurb:

> This book is about a special place, a place deep within human consciousness, a place of stillness and calm, of understanding beyond words . . . etc.

Off the page

Where do your beliefs come from?

Identify one of your core beliefs, things like:

- We are created to love;
- God is everywhere;
- This world is not my home;
- God loves me;
- There is no 'meaning' or purpose in life.

Focus on that belief and try to track where it comes from, how you came to believe it. As examples you might consider:

- I don't know, I've always believed it.
- It just seems to come from somewhere inside.
- I learnt this belief from my parents.
- It's part of my religious faith and heritage.
- I've thought it through and this is the conclusion I've come to.

Does thinking of your belief in this way strengthen it?

Prayer: rearrange the furniture

Not feng shui but the simple idea that you can pray through use of space. You can do this with any space, large or small, but more time and muscle power will be needed if you plan to reorganize a forest so we'll stick to a smaller-scale example.

First think about how objects and space can be used to point to God. Churches and cathedrals might give you some ideas, or you might think of statements like:

- God is in everything.
- God is all around.
- God is beyond.
- God is at the heart.

How could you rearrange your prayer space to reflect this? This will depend on where you are in your own spiritual journey, of course, but here are some ideas:

- Have a blank sheet of paper in the middle of your desk: the unknowable but ever-present mystery.
- Carry a small icon (bought or of your own devising) with you so that wherever you pray, you are reminded that God is there.
- Fix or paint a spot high up on the wall. Look at it as you pray and imagine your gaze going through that spot, through the wall, the air, the sky and into space. Where will your gaze travel and where will God be on that journey?
- Do the same thing with a spot at eye level and imagine your eye line following the curvature of the earth. Who would you encounter and what would your prayer be for them?
- Choose objects with different colours and textures to popu-

late the space. God made the colours and God made us able to feel. What do these objects tell you about God?

Prayer: partnership
If you want to pray for people, enter into a partnership with God. You will bring that person or group of people to God by thinking about them, concentrating on their needs and asking for specific things. For everything you ask you will agree to do something yourself. For example:

- Prayer for Joan's healing: I will write to Joan.
- Praying for disaster victims: I will become better informed about the issues.
- Praying for disaster victims: I will give some money.
- Prayer for world peace: I will enact forgiveness and peace in my life.

You might decide not to pray for anything you can't do something about.

Off the page
Do you go to a church or other religious group? In churches people deal with the very biggest questions of all, often focused on the very tiniest of protagonists – ourselves and our lives. Questions of universal creation, the fate of humanity, life and death; these mingle with our personal aches and pains, hopes and fears, joys and tragedies. It's big stuff, week after week; if ever a creative communal response were called for it is here.

So ask yourself – how creative are you in church?

Prayer: boot it upstairs

This is a continuation of 'Chair of the board' in the 'Meditation' section above. How you use it will depend on what you believe about intercessional prayer – asking God for specific outcomes.

Imagine that you are wrestling with a problem and you've used 'Chair of the board' techniques. Let's say it's a convoluted relationship issue and you're unable to see the way forward. You've listened to the part of you that's angry, the part that's confused, hurt, self-righteous, self-critical and so on. All of your 'shadows' have had their say but you can't decide how to proceed, you have no peace or 'closure' on the issue and you can't see a way forward. This might be the time to boot the problem 'upstairs' and let a higher authority deal with it. You might feel that you're leaving it in God's hands or that you're leaving it alone for a bit, allowing time and circumstance to work things out.

In order to do this effectively, you might need to represent this graphically in your imagination. Here's one version to give you the idea:

We've decided to leave this problem for now and send it to a higher authority. The issue is clearly set out in this document and I have been asked by the board to present it to the higher authority.

I walk along the silent imposing corridors from the board room. There are large solid oak doors on either side and a sense of sombre quiet about the place. I come to 'the' doors – big, solid, double doors at the end of the furthest corridor. I know what I must do and so I push open one of the doors; it moves silently on its hinges. Inside, on the dimly lit marble floor a square is marked

and it is in here that I place the document. Then I bow
and say, 'I respectfully leave this for you. I am unable to
work with it at the moment and I pray that you will.
Thank you.'

I turn and leave. As I do the door closes behind me
with a firm click. I know that I will not be able to open
it again until the time is right for me to take up this
problem afresh.

I have an example of this type of prayer working in practice. I
was wrestling with such a relationship issue and, despite a
period of 'Chair of the board' and other types of meditation I
wasn't getting anywhere. Every time I thought about what
had happened I got angry and confused. So I decided that I had
to put the issue away for a time and leave it to God until such
time as God gave it back to me. So using the technique above
I left the problem behind God's door and heard it firmly shut
behind me. Several times during the following morning I was
tempted to open the door and pick up the problem again but
each time I told myself that it was now out of my hands and I
shouldn't take it up again.

Later that morning I was reading a book for my work and a
single sentence jumped out at me, something that made me
stop and consider my issue in a fresh and helpful light. God
had given it back to me with a gift of new understanding. Or
time had done its work. Or by putting the problem away I'd
been able to concentrate on my work and see something that I
wouldn't have if my mind were still obsessed with the
problem. Or my subconscious mind was working on it all the
time, looking for a way to express a new thought. What
happened could have been any or all of these things depending
on how you interpret events.

One word of warning about this type of prayer: you can't use it for all your problems and lock them all away. It's only for those times when you need to put something to one side until you feel able to work with it again or, if your belief is such, it's for those times when you can go no further and need to leave something in God's care.

Reasons to be cheerful

Make a list of things to be thankful for and work through a few each time you pray. Dwell on each one for a few moments, thinking about the difference it makes (or has made) to your life and what life would be like without it, and give thanks for each one before moving on. Here's part of my list on the day of writing (excluding some personal items). It's made up of perennial favourites (like the first two) and some specific to the time:

- My family
- Anaesthetic at the dentist
- Recovery to health of . . .
- Reading
- Current projects
- Friends and colleagues
- Harpo Marx
- Meditation
- Today's nice surprise
- Moving on with . . .
- Good news about some new work
- Cool water
- Soft warm beds

Awe and wonder

In the same way as you did above, focus on things that inspire awe and wonder. Bring each into your prayer for a few moments and dwell on it. You could ask for a greater understanding and appreciation or to be taken deeper into the wonder and mystery (probably the same thing); or you can use it as a time to give thanks for living in a world of such awe, wonder and mystery.

Here's part of my list:

- How thought becomes action
- How music speaks
- How relationships grow
- The four-colour map problem (look it up!)
- Sleep
- Consciousness
- Colour
- Imaginative empathy

Finally, here's my prayer at the end of writing this chapter.

> Dear God
> I'm still waiting for that instant transport
>   machine.
>
> Dear Gordon,
> Close your eyes,
> Breathe deeply,
> Tense and relax your muscles . . .
> . . . now where would you like to go?

THOUGHT STARTERS

Spirituality is about inspiration, not dogma; it's about things that are unknowable but towards which we reach.

The big questions – questions of meaning, purpose and destiny – keep us moving forward in a creative way, so explorations of faith and creativity come together again.

If we think we've found 'it', we surely haven't.

All you need for somewhere to meditate is somewhere you can meditate.

Do you have the ability to 'see God in others'?

Work creatively with your uncertainties, finding new ways in, new ways of understanding that lead to a deeper, more honest type of prayer.

If I concentrate on the story, then something powerful happens.

4 ✧

The creative path of communal creativity

If you've read the rest of this book you'll be aware of my core belief that we are at our most human when we are creative. Following on from this, I believe that communities function at their best when they create together.

Community creativity manifests itself in many diverse and varied forms, from school plays to literary events and from flower festivals to communal murals. Sometimes the work is spontaneous, growing directly out of the community, such as a photography group or a school drama club; and sometimes it involves outside agencies, such as local or national arts bodies. The choices and possibilities are endless.

In this chapter I want to focus on just one mechanism for encouraging and supporting shared creativity – awaydays and events. I spend some of my time leading workshops/seminars like these for a variety of organizations and so, as elsewhere in this book, I'll be drawing on examples taken from these events.

Definitions

We should begin by defining some terms, so here's the kind of thing I'm thinking about.

'Awayday' or 'awayevent'?
These are essentially the same type of animal. 'Awayday' as a term gives a good sense of being separate from normal life and

it has a holiday feel. Its disadvantage is that it so clearly suggests a time period. So 'event' in this context means the same thing with the same kind of aims but over a longer period, often a weekend for voluntary groups such as churches or mid week for companies and other organizations. Other terms that are used include: creative break, creative retreat, awayweekend, awayevent, awaywiththefairies (this last is not necessarily a positive title . . .).

Whatever it's called, it's a time that includes some element of:

- Getting away together;
- Doing different things and doing them differently;
- Focusing on specific questions, issues or learning areas;
- Looking for explicit outcomes;
- Some relaxation;
- A chance to step aside from everyday life.

Which creative communities do you belong to? Or perhaps a better way of thinking about this is to simply ask yourself which communities you belong to because all human communities are creative – it's in our nature. Picture the dullest workplace imaginable. Perhaps it's an office environment where everything is routine and where there seems no room for any kind of creativity. What happens? People gossip, they play games, they tell jokes or build fictitious situations (such as a running gag about the boss); they subvert the formality with human, that is to say creative, responses. Gossip, for example, is essentially story-telling; elaborating, subtly changing and retelling the tale for emphasis. I'm not saying gossip is a good thing – in fact it can be deeply destructive to our humanity – but it does grow from the creative impulse, and like all such creativity it is a uniquely human response. How much better if that kind of energy could be put to use in an organization – and this is what these events try to do: create opportunities for releasing and sharing creativity.

Off the page

Where are you allowed to be your most creative? Think of all the groups and organizations you belong to. These might include: family, work, child-centred groups, church, sports teams, gym, book group ... and many more. Now draw a picture of yourself at each of these groups. Try to show by your stance and facial expression in each picture how creative you feel there. A simple stick figure will do.

An alternative is to write words that express the same thing.

Now that you know when and where you are at your most creative, you can begin to think about how you could change the way you are in the least creative group or simply attend it less – or cut it out altogether.

In this chapter I want to concentrate on three community-based opportunities for creativity, but of course there are many more possibilities. We'll look at a creativity and innovation day for an organization, the use of improvisational play for adults and then, by way of example, we'll focus in some detail on a weekend away for a church group. I hope that this last section will suggest ways in which creative events of all types can be valuable for any organization.

Creative organization day

I'd better start with a confession: I'm a real enthusiast for this kind of event. In fact, much as I love writing and production work, I'm delighted whenever I'm booked for a creative training event. At the risk of sounding un-British and unashamedly enthusiastic, I get a real kick out of working with a group and slowly seeing them take on their own creative flow. I like to get applause for what *I* do, but I absolutely love the feeling of 'Wow, look what we did!' In fact, baring my soul even more, if you believe that there's one thing everyone does well then this is it for me: helping groups to release their creativity and make something together.

Why should you think about a creative day for your organization?

- Working creatively together is great for team-building.
- You'll get new ideas and explore new ways of working.
- You'll stretch yourselves as a team.
- You'll stretch yourselves individually.
- You'll find out more about yourself and your colleagues.
- You'll learn to communicate better.
- You'll be refreshed.

There are many different approaches to creative days for organizations. Here are three.

The first is the 'guru' – someone who is an acknowledged expert in their field, a 'name' from whom the team can learn by association. Edward de Bono is a guru! Take a look at his most famous book, *Six Thinking Hats* (Penguin, 2000), to get a flavour of his approach. He helps us to think in new ways and keep our ideas fresh and our creativity active.

The second type of creative event is the 'method'. This is where you are taught a series of creative exercises and given a 'toolkit' of ideas and exercises that you can take away with you to turn to whenever you need 'creativity'. If creativity is akin to chasing a tiger through the jungle, being alert to and respond-ing to what you meet on the way and always moving forward to new territory as you chase, then the 'method' approach seems to say – here's an automated tiger trap: press the button to catch a tiger every time. It might work, but is it fun?

The third is best summed up in the word *'purposeful'*. These events have a clear aim, agreed with the team in advance, but the route to achieving that aim is left open. This is, in my opinion, the most creative approach, the most akin to other art forms. The painter has a range of skills, techniques and expe-rience but when he faces the blank canvas it is by experimen-tation, both in the mind and on the canvas, that the picture begins to form. In this analogy the painter has an end in mind but does not know how it will look in detail until it is created. The writer sits down to write and the creation takes place as she does so, building on her thoughts and experience as she goes. Working in this way can be risky, scary and wonderfully rewarding.

None of these approaches involves any 'con', and what the participants get is an experience of creativity, an experience of their own creativity. But if that all sounds too esoteric, remem-ber that it's rooted in the aims of the event. Here are some of the aims that I've worked with recently:

- To foster new approaches to creativity;
- To help us to work together more effectively;
- To find creative approaches to flexible working and work life balance;

- To get us thinking 'out of the box', finding new ways to approach our daily tasks;
- To come up with some new programme ideas;
- To develop innovative multimedia ideas;
- To think creatively about how our organization uses the Web;
- To improve our communication skills;
- To better understand writing for the Web.

Off the page

To help you focus on areas that you could creatively work on, take the organization's logo and redraw it to reflect your feelings about the organization. So if, for example, the logo has bright letters, you might draw them tarnished and a little rusty, or you might repeat the logo over and over again to represent the way that things are stuck in a rut – always doing the same thing.

You can also have some creative fun with the organization's slogan – 'We make a difference' could become 'We make no difference', or 'We make a difference but it's always the same difference', or 'We bake a biscuit (stale)'.

I wrote earlier that I believe that creativity is its own reward and needs no other reason to exist; it's an important part of being human and we are 'created to be creative'. Now I seem to be saying that creativity must be tied to a purpose, a definite and defined aim. The difference is context. In a work or organization environment (such as a club or voluntary work), the community exists for some other function – to make buttons, films, dinners; to develop skills, to worship together, to learn . . .

In these contexts, a creativity event (which is likely to cost some hard-earned money) has to fit the aims of the organization. Having said that, there is nothing wrong with an organization deciding that the aim for a particular day is 'to have some fun together' or 'to share a learning experience together'. An aim of this kind can be valuable in itself; equally a specific outcome-based day, such as 'improving communications between technical and production staff', is also legitimate and valuable. So this is the third type of creative day that might be expected: working creatively together towards some stated aim.

What might happen on such a day? That will depend entirely on the organization, the agreed aims and other factors, such as the time available, space, size of group, and so on. The truth is that I find it difficult to write about what happens on a creative day of the third kind for two reasons.

1 You need to keep things flexible and have a variety of ideas to choose from; some of these are vague to say the least and are developed as we go along – it's called creativity.
2 When people ask in advance – 'What's going to happen on "on the day"?', I tend to respond in a general way because I've learnt that any idea can sound flat and dull until you put it on its feet and do it for real. Saying that 'You're going to be drawing your programme as if it were a cereal packet', or 'You'll be working using dreams as a metaphor' can be off-putting, with people responding that this is 'not my sort of thing'.

The day is really about building slowly, sensitively and going with the group. Every good workshop leader knows that the most valuable thing they bring is their antennae and their judgement to interpret the signals they pick up. Even after years of experience, I find it hard to start a creative session with a new group. There's always a point where I start listening to myself and thinking, 'You're not grabbing them. They haven't a clue what you're talking about.' Experience has taught me to press on because it's true, they don't know what I'm talking about and they won't until they start to experience creative working for themselves. As soon as we get into the first creative exercise, the day really begins and, step by step, we start to work together in new and engaging ways.

Usually the first activity is something easily accessible, often with a fun element. A favourite is the jargon auction, which works like this:

1 Work with the delegates to build a list of jargon expressions commonly used in the organization, at least ten examples.
2 Enjoy the groans and moans as the annoying examples are written up and briefly explained.
3 Give out chocolate money to use in the auction – for some reason this mostly seems to work out at 42p each (the shade of Douglas Adams in evidence, perhaps?).
4 Explain that delegates can bid for items of jargon and whatever they buy they own for the day. If anyone else uses that jargon during the day, the owner gets a point. The delegate with the most points at the end of the day wins a prize (usually chocolate).
5 Begin the bidding and have some fun!

This is mainly aimed at breaking the ice and getting people engaged at the beginning of the session but it also makes the point (and I make sure to make the point) that jargon can be a block to creativity. If you always talk in the same limited way with the same restricted vocabulary, there's not a lot of room for creative engagement. Banishing jargon from a creative day is a good start. Mind you, on more than one occasion delegates have later taken me to task for my jargon – they soon learn my stock phrases and pick up on them!

Off the page

Devise your own fun game with a serious point. Something related to your work that will enable people to have fun together and to start thinking about the issues in a light, enjoyable way.

To get you thinking, take a few moments each day to step back and look objectively at what goes on, the routines and behaviour patterns of the working environment – does this give you inspiration for a game? It could, for example, be a quiz based on some of these aspects of routine and behaviour.

The day then proceeds with a variety of activities, some of which are based on the frames exercises described in Chapter 3; others are related specifically to the delegates' concerns. These might include script-writing, role play, listening and responding to stories (being read to is a wonderful experience and something we should all have more of), expressing ideas graphically and so on. Nothing very surprising or unusual there; the key is to find that slightly different angle that will take people off into new ways of thinking without leading them to feel lost or anxious. Let me give one brief example to illustrate this.

I worked on a one-day session with a creative team in broadcasting. The day had gone well and everyone was enjoying themselves and coming up with lots of new ideas but I had a feeling that somehow it all felt like an exercise that wasn't going to have a huge impact on their working lives after the day. Certainly some of the programming ideas would feed into their offers process but once those ideas had run their course I felt that the day's usefulness wouldn't go much further. I started to pick up that the words 'time' and 'space' kept coming up – not a reference to *Dr Who* but a very clear message that what this group mainly needed wasn't help with creativity in relation to their work (after all they were all creative people responsible for some great innovations and programmes); what they needed was to find creative uses for their time in order to be able to let their creativity run free, unfettered by office procedure, targets, their commissioning system, and so on.

What had started as a day focusing on creative broadcasting became a day about creative time management. After a coffee break, I put to the delegates the idea that we should bring all their considerable creativity to bear on this issue. They should all step into the shoes of the most creative managers (they didn't like thinking of themselves in this way – management were 'the enemy' to some extent); and really tackle this problem. We used role play and framing exercises to get to grips with the issues and see them in a new light. Trying to see things from management's point of view was particularly revelatory. The outcome was a list of short-term achievable goals and longer-term aims, broken down into steps – all with the clear focus of cutting the bureaucracy and freeing the programme-makers to – guess what – make programmes!

Off the page

What is the character of your organization, group or club? Imagine it is a person. How old would it be? Male or female? And what kind of looks and personality would it have?

Once you've thought about this, go shopping for clothes for it. Get hold of some catalogues and magazines and cut out the kind of clothes you think your organization should wear. They can be different styles to reflect different parts, divisions or moods (formal wear, casual wear, even night wear!).

When you've dressed the organization, give him or her a name.

Consider what this tells you about the organization and what things you might want to change.

One of my favourite creative organization days is a team-building exercise – 'Radio play in a day'. This clearly builds on my experience as a radio drama producer, opening up the magic of this kind of drama for everyone. It is very much for those who are not usually involved in broadcast media; management teams from any organization, for example. There are a range of skills to learn, both technical and artistic (and many that are both – where does creating the sound of someone being sick fall?); and there's an emphasis on good collaborative team work from the word go. The buzz at this kind of event is wonderful and the creative tension in the studio and control room as we all race against the clock to get our programme completed on time is a real 'high'. To my mind this is a far more powerful form of team-building than trying to build a bridge across a river or making a raft out of oil drums. 'Radio play in a day' stretches people's abilities and opens up new possibilities. It's entirely collaborative and the end result is something to take away and be proud of.

Off the page

What are the occasions when you let yourself 'off the leash' of respectable adulthood and simply allow yourself to play? Do you ever run wildly down a hill swinging your arms with joy as you did when a child? Do you enjoy paddling in the sea or a river? Try to identify any areas of your life that are simply playing, improvising, making things up without too many rules. If you can't think of anything, see what you can plan. There's no need to challenge yourself to go beyond your comfort zone; just take a small simple step into the world of play. You could:

- Build a mud pie (surreptitiously while gardening);
- Draw beards and moustaches on respectable people in newspapers (the *Church Times* is always defaced in this way in our house);
- Start answering the radio back with irreverent comments;
- Have a little private dance in your own room;
- Get out some old clothes and play dressing-up;
- Write a wild adventure story or romance just for yourself.

Whatever the activities and aims, however you have worked, and no matter what the outcomes, always try to keep the last hour of your awayday as a time of reflection on the day and an opportunity to suggest some ways forward. That last hour is always a valuable time and on many occasions I've been grateful to have it there so that ideas and questions we pick up during the day can be parked and returned to then. And, of course, there's always the result of the jargon auction and the prize-giving to end on.

Improvisation

I love to play and one type of adult play is called 'improvisation'. I run workshops where anyone can come and explore different themes such as dreams, 'I want to be' (playing at being someone else), and so on. These sessions are really pure self-indulgence on my part, but I do think there's tremendous value in playing 'as if', in putting yourself in someone else's shoes; whether for 'fun', self-development and understanding; or for a more specific purpose, the latter usually in a work context.

This is one extreme of the use of drama; it's focused solely on improvisational play, is for a diverse group of interested people and has no other aim than providing opportunities for this kind of experience. At the more practical and focused end, the model of drama strategies, of forms and styles developed in educational drama, provides valuable tools when working with adults, particularly in training and development contexts. Many companies use 'role play' in their training programmes and this is a useful learning exercise. You can apply the principles of educational drama to extend this learning. These principles are:

- To see things from someone else's point of view;
- To reflect on courses of action;

- To reflect on thoughts, feelings and reactions;
- To learn from others in a collaborative fashion.

In order to achieve this, educational dramatists use various strategies, which often focus on creating a distance between the event and the learner so that they are enabled to look at and reflect on what has happened.

Let's take an example. An airline is training its check-in staff to deal with difficult customers and they use role play with one person taking the part of the member of staff and the other being a customer who has missed their check-in time by five minutes and is demanding to be let on the plane late. The normal procedure would be to run the improvisation and then talk about it, drawing out the strong and weak points of how the member of staff handled the situation. Here are some brief suggestions for how educational drama strategies could be useful.

Speaking thoughts
Stop the improvisation at any significant point and ask the participants what they (their roles) are thinking, before returning to the scene. This helps all the course delegates to think about how thought patterns affect behaviour. For example, the member of staff might be thinking, 'Here comes trouble', as soon as the customer arrives and this may shape the whole subsequent conversation.

Swap
Ask the participants to swap roles during the improvisation. This is a very clear way of seeing things from someone else's point of view. You can also swap-in course members who are watching the improvisation. Having discussed how it's going

at a particular point and having heard people's suggestions for what the member of staff should do next, let individuals try out their ideas by becoming that role.

Draw it out

Take either of the participants and ask them to lie on a large piece of paper, either on the floor or against a wall. Draw around their outline, and then allow them to move away. The whole group can then write comments on the outline to facilitate further discussion. One focus might be to draw out the different pressures acting on the member of staff by surrounding their outline with comments such as, 'Worried about home situation', 'Tired and working late', 'Feeling pressure to be calm', 'Nervous of the possibility of violence' . . . and so on.

Pictures and captions

Having run the improvisation, ask the participants to pick the significant moments from the encounter and present them as captioned pictures. The pictures can be drawn or 'still pictures' (tableaux with participants freezing in position). Captions might include: 'Here comes trouble', 'Why doesn't she understand?', 'It's only ten minutes' . . . You can run this exercise with everyone else as well, working in pairs.

These are just a few of the possible strategies but I hope they demonstrate the richness of these techniques in training and development situations.

Church awaydays

In the final section of this chapter I want to focus on away-events for groups and societies and use churches and church groups as an example. As I said earlier, I hope that this exploration will be of use, whatever groups you're involved in. I'm going to do this mainly by telling the story of an imaginary event (using examples and experiences drawn from real life but not a description of one single event) and by focusing on what the participants think and feel. There will also be other examples as appropriate along the way.

St Jude's are having a weekend away – Friday evening to Sunday lunchtime. Marion is 36 and this is what she thinks as she set off:

> This is a familiar feeling – I don't want to go, but I know I will probably get something out of it. At the moment I wish I wasn't going but last year I started to feel more positive as we got halfway there, so I'm hoping for the same this year. There are always some good bits and I'm looking forward to having a chance to chat to some people in the bar – Amanda became a real friend after last year and I'd like to make friends among some of the newer people. I could do without the food, though – it's always terrible for vegetarians.

Yuri is 25:

> I've never been on one of these things before and I'm really looking forward to it. I want to get a puppet group started at the church and I think this weekend could be the catalyst for that. I only hope it's not taken over by the boring old ****s who seem to run everything at St Jude's, but I guess it's up to me to make a stand about that.

Roger is 58:

> I do wonder if I'm getting a bit old for these weekends
> in a kind of 'old dog, new tricks' sort of way. I'm very
> keen that the church should move forward and I don't
> want us old lags running the thing for ever. The trick
> with these weekends (and I must admit we've had some
> good ones in the past) is to enjoy them for what they are
> and then try to get something worthwhile for the growth
> of the church out of them. I'm sorry that Rosemarie [his
> wife] wasn't able to come. She's seemed distant of late. I
> hope I don't spend the whole time worrying about her.

We'll be coming back to Marion, Yuri and Roger later in the
chapter, but for now, let's take a quick look at their expecta-
tions to help define the essential qualities of this kind of event.

It's different
Each of our participants is aware, in some way, that this is not
going to be 'life as we know it' – this is something out of the
ordinary.

It's challenging
Each of the three is concerned at the very least, perhaps even a
little fearful. Roger wonders if he's getting too old and his
thoughts betray an awareness that things are changing at St
Jude's. Yuri is concerned about whether his voice will be heard
and he's nervous about his particular agenda, which he
expresses in terms of a puppet group, but this could be simply
him wanting to make his mark as a 'younger person'. Marion
is probably nervous of her own feelings. As she says, she's been
here before and she has a mixture of emotions as she sets out.

There's anticipation
All three hope for something good from at least part of the event.

It's a genesis
The hope for something new, of long-term significance, is on the agenda of all three. Marion hopes to make lasting friendships; Yuri hopes to start his puppet group and become more involved; Roger wants to see younger people take a lead role and hopes for 'something worthwhile for the growth of the church'.

It's varied
Despite the similarities, Marion, Yuri and Roger each look for a different experience from the weekend.

It's connected
Although this is an 'away time', set aside from everyday life, each of them brings their world and concerns to the weekend. Roger is concerned about his relationship with his wife; Yuri has issues about the older people in the church; and Marion brings concerns about friendship and, reading between the lines, her own shyness.

The thoughts and feelings of these three participants give us another perspective. Whatever the focus and nature of the awayday or event, participants will probably approach it with a sense of something different that is challenging. There'll be a degree of anticipation and a hope for a genesis – a new beginning – yet each will have their own varied hopes and fears around the event and they remain connected to the rest of their lives, bringing their concerns with them.

Off the page

Daydream the ideal event for your organization, group or club. What would you be aiming to achieve?

If you could go anywhere, where would you go?

If you could have any speakers and session leaders who would they be (think either of actual people you know or of qualities they might possess)?

What would happen at the event?

How would people be changed by it?

What difference would it make to the organization?

You could use these thoughts to help you plan a real event, taking the ideas and seeing how realizable they are in practice.

Two examples

We'll return to St Jude's soon, but let's break off to look at some other church-based awaydays and events to get a picture of how they worked and what they achieved. Again these are based on real events.

Two into one

Two churches were combining under a single vicar. We'll call them St Paul's and St Thecla's. Their new vicar, the Revd Graham Freshman, wanted to create a joint vision for the future so he set up an awayday. It was to be a single day – a Saturday. He brought in a facilitator (not me!) to help the small planning team think through the event – an experienced and creative person who gave his time for free (definitely not me). There were tensions in the planning group mainly around the question of vision. Graham

Freshman wanted the day to be about the two churches lifting their eyes from their current difficulties (the union was a painful one – an economic marriage, not a love match); but some of the planning group couldn't think beyond questions such as, how they were to share the vicar, who was to produce the magazine and who would pay for what. Will Power – the facilitator – quickly recognized these tensions and, working closely with the vicar, devised a programme aimed at taking everyone forward. He built sessions based on group work, including:

- Modelling the future of the church using plants and moss, twigs, etc.;
- Creative artistic activities for children – craft and drama;
- Writing a song celebrating the qualities of the churches;
- Writing church council minutes of five years hence;
- Establishing aims and objectives for different areas of the churches' lives.

This was an effective day and worked on the principles of 'something for everyone', and 'something familiar, something strange'. The 'familiar' included formal times of worship, small group discussions and a visit from the bishop. This last wasn't necessarily normal but it was familiar – a church-type activity. The 'strange' was all the creative ways of working, which were new to many of the participants.

There was a lot packed into the day and the results were varied, as was the enthusiasm with which different people responded, but everyone got something out of it and the aims of bringing people together and looking for a vision for the future were at least partly met. The idea very quickly emerged that a significant part of the vision (enabling growth and joint commitment) would be focusing on young families and the young people of the church for whom there was little provision. Much of this shared vision was eroded over the months and years that followed and the bright hopes of that day were not realized in reality – except for one small group. On that day some church members made a commitment to set up a group for the young people of both churches. This group was formed and met regularly for the following five years. It was always small in number but the young people involved were very committed and, as the older ones left, new members were eager to join. The group made a difference in their lives and it all grew out of a shared creative vision and commitment at an awayday.

Out of the box

This was a creative weekend with lay workers from a number of churches in a diocese. There were about 30 participants and I was brought in quite late in the day, after the previous speaker had to pull out. I'm not a 'speaker' in the sense that is normally understood in these contexts – someone with a 'message' to share. I'm more of an event leader; as I mention elsewhere I get the greatest joy from enabling creativity and releasing it in others. I think the event organizer took a deep breath before she agreed to my plans for the weekend. She knew it would not be what the participants were expecting. We looked at everything 'out of the box' including worship, 'the word', thinking, praying, music and more. The weekend was divided into the following sessions:

Friday evening: stepping out of the box
Introduction of the theme.
Simple drama activity – still pictures (tableaux), showing the life of the church.

Introduction of the weekend's theme – the story of Lazarus (he came out of the box!).

Praying out of the box – imaginative prayer activity using boxes.

Saturday morning 1: worship out of the box
Introducing the main work of the weekend. There was a communion service planned for Sunday morning and different groups took responsibility for sections of the worship:

- Welcome
- Music
- Prayer
- Reading
- Teaching
- Communion
- Taking creativity away with us

Each group was encouraged to think of all the senses as they prepared and to come up with original and refreshing ways of presenting their section. The groups had time in this session and later in the day to prepare their input.

Saturday morning 2: the word out of the box
This session offered different inputs – a dancer, a partially sighted person, a storyteller, and someone who worked with mentally disabled young people. The aim was to get a creative look at 'the word' from a different perspective.

I had to leave that afternoon and evening to attend a prior engagement. While I was away the participants had business meetings and an evening entertainment in addition to working on their creative input.

Sunday morning

To give a break from the frenetic creative activity, we had a
session on work life balance just before the worship. This is an
area that the event organizer was very keen to include in the
programme.

Worship

The fruits of all their labours! Each group had really taken the
message to heart and stepped right out of the box. The welcoming group, for example, started at breakfast that morning with
flowers for every delegate and continued throughout the
morning with images, words and smells! The music included
traditional singing and music with the words projected so that
we read (but didn't sing) as we listened – this gave the words
and music freshness. I won't run through results from every
group, but I do want to mention two in particular. When it
came to 'the word' – that is teaching or preaching – I was
initially disappointed. There were three short sermons on the
story of Lazarus and none of them seemed to me to match the
punch of the innovative, dramatized reading we had just seen.
Then came a surprise: the section ended with a short reading –
from the Koran. With this particular group, this was radical
stuff, prompted in the aftermath of 11 September 2001. It was
a brave step – right out of the box of the orthodoxy in which
I'd assumed some of them lived and it was a powerful and
thought-provoking creative moment.

The other group that I want to mention is the communion
group. They developed something that was entirely original,
involving no bread or wine or food of any sort. It probably
loses its impact when written down, but for me it was a powerful testament to the unlocking of creativity. We all sat in a
circle with a large space in the centre. Some words about the

death of Christ were spoken and, as they were, large sheets of paper were torn from a flip chart; the effect was powerful, the ripping sound and action were dramatic. The action and sounds produced that classic drama effect – high impact creating a tension in us all; anticipation, uncertainty and nervousness as to where it was going, and a heightened sense of engagement. The large sheets were placed to form a giant cross on the floor. A sheet was added on top to represent Christ. Thick red paint was poured over the 'president's' hands and she then smeared the topmost piece of paper, which was then folded in on itself so that the paint spread across the whole sheet, creating a smudged red surface. Again this was drama in the raw – powerful, and engaging the brain and the emotions. The final act involved tearing the paper into small pieces and giving one to each participant. The drama had come to each one of us – a smaller-scale, more personal connection.

How does this strike you? Odd? Unusual? Perhaps even inappropriate? But it is no more strange than giving people a wafer or a small piece of bread and saying, 'This is my body . . . eat it.'

Creativity helps us to take the familiar and see it from a new perspective, and all the participants in this particular weekend achieved this. I should point out that this was genuinely a joint effort. I was simply part of the team that made it happen – all of the creative responses came from the participants themselves.

Back to St Jude's

Now let's see how Marion, Yuri and Roger are getting on. The focus for their weekend is 'My story' – reflecting on personal pilgrimage:

- Where we came from;
- Where we are now;
- Where we want to be.

It is mid-afternoon on Saturday, and Yuri and Marion have discovered a common interest in puppetry – they're now deep in conversation, some might say plotting, as they hatch plans to set up a puppet group at St Jude's. They had started talking in the bar the previous evening after the first session, which was about remembering childhood dreams and aspirations. Marion had fondly remembered her childhood puppet theatre; she had talked briefly in the session about how speaking through puppets had helped her overcome shyness and allowed her to perform. They've found the rest of the weekend so far pretty good, but their main focus is their new venture. There's no doubt about it, St Jude's is going to have a puppet group!

In contrast, Roger is quieter than usual. He's not said much in the sessions, but he has found them moving, rather unbearably so. They've brought to the surface some of his thoughts about his wife and how, just recently, they've rather lost contact. He knows the title of the next session is 'Where we want to be' and he knows that his personal answer is 'home'.

The sessions have been quietly and sensitively led; there's been an opportunity to use all sorts of different media and a range of responses, but no pressure to 'perform'. This has not been a showbiz type of creativity, yet the sessions have gently moved people on and made connections – both between and within people.

Off the page

Take some time to appreciate your friends and relations, either present or in the past. Choose one person to think about.

- What makes them special?
- What is it about that person that you like, respect and appreciate?
- Think about your earliest memory of that person – how has your relationship changed over time?

Make a decision to think about that person over the coming week, celebrating them and your friendship. If appropriate, say a prayer of thanks for their life. Another way of remembering them during the week is to assign a particular sight or event as a memory-jogger. You might, for example, decide that every time you look at your watch you will think of the time you first met; or you might choose to think of contacting them whenever you write an email or pick up a letter.

The session leader, Geoff, seeks Roger out – his antennae tell him something's moving. He gives Roger time and suggests that he does go home. They talk quietly for a while and the next session is late starting. Yuri and Marion use the extra time for a spot of networking . . .

We'll leave St Jude's for now and come back later to see how things have developed.

Off the page
Create a collage, draw a picture, write a poem or respond
in any way you feel appropriate to the word 'home'.

What does home represent for you – is it a place, a
feeling, a group of people . . . ?

If appropriate, make your item small enough to carry
with you as a reminder of home wherever you are.

Planning an awayday or event

Let's imagine that a group you're involved with wants to put
together an event or day, one which uses creative approaches.
What are the things you need to think about? Here's a check-
list of some of the questions you'll need to consider:

- Why – what's it for? The aim.
- What specific outcomes are we anticipating?
- Who is it for? How long? What kind of place should we go
  to?
- What kind of leadership does the event call for? Will we
  book an outside facilitator?
- What kind of sessions will there be? The programme.
- What are the next practical steps we need to take?

A few notes on each of these:

The aim
I was a trainee teacher in the dim, distant past. I approached
this task as I'd approached my whole education, with a kind of
calmly arrogant 'I can do this' approach. I relied on my ability

to think creatively on my feet. Or, to put it another way, I was dead lazy. For every lesson, we students had to produce a lesson plan and right up there at the top was always 'aim'. I got away with the old dodge of looking in my file when the tutor turned up to watch a lesson, 'I'm sure it's here somewhere', then hastily writing it up at home afterwards and bringing it in the next day. I admit I was a terrible student, yet I think that I was a reasonable teacher. In truth, the whole business of writing an aim seemed a little artificial to me. I knew what I was about – engaging the children's interest, surviving, having a good time, looking for moments of creative spark and energy . . . but I couldn't put any of this under 'aim'. The specific aim might be about writing poems inspired by rubbish (hey, this was the 1970s, none of that grammar nonsense), but it always had to be dressed up in circuitous language. It was never enough to say, 'Get them thinking and writing', but that was really what it was about. Was it really better to say: 'To use a stimulus from everyday waste to kindle creative responses, shared and developed into well-structured and meaningful poetry'?

Tirade over, but the point is, be real about your aims and objectives. If you're really thinking that it would just be nice to get away together, get to know people better and enjoy working with each other, that's fine. It's much better to have this kind of aim than something waffly and grand-sounding. In many corporate situations the aim of the aim is to demonstrate our command of key jargon and to sound ever so slightly confusing – you don't understand, maybe one day you'll join the ranks of those of us who do! Of course, the church or your voluntary group is not into that sort of thing, is it?

Here are some possible aims for any awayday or event:

- To share some time together and get to know each other better;
- To bring different parts of the organization together;
- To unlock creative gifts;
- To undertake a radical review of pedagogical hierarchies in relation to community-centred issues connected to age-related cultural structures;
- To use creativity in learning and development;
- To make long/medium-term plans for the future;
- To address specific issues (could be anything – leadership structures, buildings issues, family support, support for singles, disability issues, giving, children . . .).

I slipped a corporate-speak wildcard in there, but you probably didn't notice.

Outcomes

Closely connected to aims are the outcomes you'd like to result from the event. As an example, an aim for a church might be: To look at service structures – can we do more for families with young children?

What kind of outcomes might you be expecting from an awayevent with this aim? Here are some possibilities:

- A better understanding of the role and nature of 'family services';
- A number of suggested patterns of worship;
- Some fresh ideas on how to engage children;
- To be challenged in our orthodoxy and assumptions.

Note that these don't do the work of the event. You're not prejudging the results, rather you're creating some empty rooms, which you'll attempt to furnish as you work together. You also need to be open to the possibility that the event will throw up ideas for new rooms, perhaps a garden, or even the demolition of some rooms. In other words, keep creative and be prepared, as you work together, for your creativity to take you into uncharted territory.

Who, where and when?

The 'who's it for' question is often implicitly answered in the initial idea to hold an event. These things often grow out of the needs of a particular group – church council, committee, young people's groups, etc. It is worth taking some time, however, to think through the constituency and maybe bring in groups, or even individuals, that you didn't first think of. Creativity can be enhanced by getting the right mix of people and by putting together unusual combinations representing different groups or viewpoints. You'll also need to think about the ideal number of people. In practical terms this will affect the venue; and in relation to creativity and learning, you'll need to think through how the participants will break down into working groups. This is my take on ideal group size but it is not based on any research, just what feels right for me.

Lecture-style presentation
Any number providing all can see and hear.

Presentation with 'audience' feedback
Depends very much on the space used – can participants be heard?

Seminar discussion
Up to 20 or thereabouts sitting in a circle.

Small group discussion
Pairs – good for a quick chat in the middle of a seminar or presentation. 'Turn to the person sitting next to you.'

Three to five are good numbers for a more extended discussion.

Creative working groups
For drama, creating resources, planning, etc. – break the whole group down into groups of three, four or five.

As to where the event takes place, you'll need to think about:

- Somewhere that is 'away'; not our usual hall (someone else's hall is fine);
- Sufficiently close for everyone to get to;
- Sufficiently far to give that all-important sense of journeying to somewhere new or different;
- Practical considerations – rooms, working spaces, etc.;
- Somewhere inspiring – if possible go to a building that's going to feed creativity in some way, perhaps with pleasant grounds or a specific architectural style;
- Somewhere that's near an interesting place, if possible. It's great to give people time off to explore Bath or Glasgow or New York State, for example.

The question of when is also about 'how long'. Should you go for a day (usually a Saturday) or for longer, such as a weekend? One-day or weekend events are quite different in nature. The creative juices can really start to flow at a weekend because, on the whole, people relax more and become less attached to the everyday and more committed to the event. That being said, weekends are more expensive in money, time and commitment, and you may get more takers for a single day. If you're very clear about what you want to achieve, a day can give great value. The decision about 'how long' will be influenced by:

- What you want to achieve;
- What you can afford;
- What is practical.

It may be, for example, that having an outside facilitator or leader for one day is a better use of time and money than having a whole weekend that you run yourselves.

This raises the other 'who' question – leadership. There are advantages to bringing in an outside facilitator or leader:

- They can be objective and look with fresh eyes;
- People respond in a different way to a 'professional stranger', they are often more willing to become involved;
- Everyone from the organization comes with the same status;
- They bring specific skills in running events.

The possible disadvantages include the danger of getting the wrong person and the expense of using someone who makes a living from this sort of thing. Whether to use a professional or home-grown talent is a decision that will be influenced by who is available, what you want to achieve and financial considerations.

Off the page

If you've been a member of a group or organization for a long time, draw a timeline with one end representing when you joined and the other end representing now. Using words, simple diagrams or a mixture of both, chart the changes that you have experienced. Show outward events such as a change of leader or a period of rapid growth or decline. Alongside this, chart the feel of the group as you see it. Perhaps you could use lines of different colours representing qualities such as friendly, organized, aimless, purposeful, etc.

The programme

Planning your event is the vital groundwork before you can grow anything or, to return to an earlier metaphor, it's finding the bare rooms which the event will furnish. Everyone needs a structure for their event – even someone like me who loves to improvise and take things in unexpected directions. You'll need to think about the following:

- Welcoming;
- Easing people across the threshold from everyday life to 'special time';
- A variety of different ways of working (see below);
- Time in groups of different sizes;
- Relaxation – time off;
- Fun;
- Practical business stuff;
- Time and space to allow creativity to flourish.

I particularly want to mention working in different ways, because for me this is crucial to the success of any event. The standard method of engaging people with ideas in churches, organizations and in education is the lecture, talk or sermon. Yet this often powerful and effective method doesn't work equally well for all people. I have a very short concentration span for this sort of thing, yet I can write a book for hours on end, and I'm often disappointed when a two-hour creative working session comes to an end. The key message is that everyone's different, and your event plan needs to take account of this. You can support different working and learning styles by creating an event that includes:

- Small group discussion;
- Seminars;
- Creative working time;
- Individual working/thinking time;
- Guided meditation;
- Different types of input – lecture, video, audio, quiet reading.

Try to include inputs for all types, not forgetting to make these age-appropriate for children and those who've been brought up with a more formal education (and those, like me, educated in the 1960s, with a more liberal approach!).

Practical steps

The stepping stones to setting up and running an awayday or event involve thinking about all the issues raised above. You might also like to talk to others who've been involved in similar events to get ideas for contacts, venues, programme possibilities and so on. To end this section here are a couple of creative exercises that you can do at an early planning meeting to help you think through your aims and the nature of the event.

How will you advertise the event?

This will require you to think about the name (and thus the aim), who you're aiming it at, and the style of the event as portrayed by any leaflets, logos, etc. Let the planning group doodle together, creating poster and logo ideas, and brainstorming names.

Feeding into the life of the organization

How do you think the event will affect the ongoing life of the organization? Will it be a one-off or lead to other things? Play a game of 'One year later' (you can also do 'Five years later'). The planning group add their suggestions to a flip chart with 'One year later' as the heading. They each write down the possible outcomes from the event. Encourage them to think in a creative way and have some fun among the serious points. Here's the result from one such brainstorm from a church group:

'One year later'

- All-age drama is a regular part of our worship.
- The all-age drama group is writing its own material.
- New young families are coming to church regularly.
- There's less tension between the choir and the drama group.
- All members of the drama group welcome children as a matter of course.
- The vicar is convinced she should be an actor – her husband says she already is.

St Jude's – one last time

To end, let's hear from Roger, Yuri and Marion as they look back at St Jude's' creative weekend six months later.

Roger

I wondered if I was getting a bit old for these weekends but that wasn't it at all. I was really wondering if I was getting a bit old, full stop! Everything I hear suggests that the weekend continued to go well after I left but my main feeling is gratitude that Geoff [event leader] persuaded me to go home because I found my wife in bed with a 25-year-old stud . . . Not really, just practising my creative/imaginative side! What really happened is that Rosemarie was shocked to see me and was convinced that I'd stormed out of the weekend. When I explained she was tremendously relieved. As we talked the whole thing came out. She told me that I'd been getting increasingly moody and she was worried about me. This explained the distance I felt between us because she didn't feel able to talk to me about it. The result was that I went to the doctor's. It turns out that I do have some mild depression and the doctor is helping me to treat it (creating stories is part of the treatment as I've joined a writing group). It's a funny thing but that creative weekend did turn out to be a creative time for me, but most importantly it gave me time and space to think.

Yuri

The weekend was brilliant. The speaker was good. Some of the activities were great, others I could take or leave to be honest, but the best thing was that we got our puppet group started. Marion is brilliant. She's really organized and when she operates one of the puppets she really becomes a different person. This was the most creative event I've ever been on – and it's really made a difference to the church because of the puppet group. I'm looking forward to next year – I'm on the planning group and there'll be a special puppet party on the Saturday night.

Marion

This was the best weekend our church has been on. I thought that the 'creative' bit might all get a bit much but in fact it was just right. I think that having creative stuff to do, which was enjoyable and challenging, took the focus away from ourselves and our concerns. As a learning method I thought it was brilliant. I'm pleased about the puppet group too – it's great to have Yuri so enthusiastic but I think his ego's a bit strong on occasions! The vegetarian food was as disastrous as usual. Now if only someone could get creative there!

THOUGHT STARTERS

Communities function at their best when they create together.

There is great value in getting away together.

Which creative communities do you belong to?

Creativity is refreshing.

Working creatively you are always moving forward to new territory.

Any idea can sound flat and dull until you put it on its feet.

Every good workshop leader knows that the most valuable thing they bring is their antennae and their judgement to interpret the signals they pick up.

Jargon can be a block to creativity.

Step back to get the bigger picture.

Find time and space to let creativity run free.

There's tremendous value in playing 'as if', in putting yourself in someone else's shoes.

A good event offers 'something for everyone', and 'something familiar, something strange'.

Creativity helps us to take the familiar and see it from a new perspective.

Planning your event is the vital groundwork before you can grow anything.

Everyone's different and your event plan needs to take account of this.

5 ✧

The creative path of wholeness

In this final chapter I want to suggest that you chart for yourself a creative path of wholeness and to do this I want to introduce a new and perhaps surprising word: discipline. With apologies to those of you who might be anticipating something spicier, I'm using discipline in relation to creating a rule for you to live by, rather as religious institutions have done through the years. I want to introduce the idea that you can create a discipline to:

- Know yourself;
- Go beyond yourself;
- Learn to live with others;
- Practise creative living.

The idea is to give some structure and order to your use of creativity, to help you to think about what you are trying to achieve. This does not deny you your spontaneity, neither does it enable you to 'be creative' at the flick of a mental switch. It does something rather more subtle than that; it allows you to apply your creativity to the process of developing a way of living, a way of moving towards wholeness.

This chapter is structured in a more formal way than previous chapters as it mainly consists of a step-by-step plan for developing your own creative approaches to wholeness. For this reason there are no 'off the page' or 'thought starter' sections here with their ad hoc approach. Rather the practical suggestions are integrated into the main text and marked consecutively as exercises.

Why wholeness?

Individuals and groups have always looked for ways to organize and discipline their lives both for the health of the individual and the good of the group. In the Christian tradition the focus has been on holiness: getting closer to what God wants you to be. Wholeness has become the new holiness for many. I use the term because it has a wider applicability than holiness, is more in tune with my understanding of creativity and is likely to be more acceptable and meaningful to a wider range of people.

Finding time

As suggested at the beginning of this chapter, in order to pursue a path of greater wholeness, you need to develop a rule or discipline; basically a structure that will help you forward. A structure is necessary because you will need to allow time for this work, you will need to assess where you are on the path and you will need to plan where you will go next. A structure is also important because it signals that this is important to you, not an idle fad that you can drop at any time; though, of course, in the spirit of creativity you'll not want to be too rigid so that you turn down a chance to see a play or meet a friend because you've planned to do some creative thinking that evening. Think of a diet or an exercise regime: in each case you need to put in the time, effort and disciplined action you need in order to achieve your goals. This creative work is similar but it is more flexible, considerably so. In fact in order to get started you need only find about ten minutes a day and even this can be flexible; sometimes you'll need a space where you can write or draw but at other times it can be thinking time while travelling or last thing at night.

I don't want to minimize, however, the difficulties that some people have with finding time for this sort of thing. Many parents, particularly those with young children, find that although they might have a few minutes of 'down time' at intervals throughout the day, they can't 'switch off' from their responsibilities enough to do this kind of work; those who work long hours and are too tired when they get home are in a similar position. In the end, working creatively is like anything else in life: if you really want to achieve something you will find a way to work on it. As I say above, you really can start with just ten minutes a day and even this doesn't have to be every day.

Exercise 1 Finding time

Work out how you are going to find two reasonably peaceful, ten-minute (longer if possible) slots, one a day over the next two days. Try to make at least one of them time when you can jot down some thoughts. The ideal is to always be able to write notes but this is not essential.

Tip: if you can't possibly think how you'll find the time, read the next section (Exercise 2) now and then put the book away and use the time you would have spent reading to work through the exercise, taking as long (or as many sessions) as you need. Then pick up the book again and read on, amazed and invigorated by your ability to find the time to put creativity into action!

Exercise 2 Considering wholeness

Take some time to consider your understanding of wholeness. You can use any of the techniques in this book, such as meditation, imagining a dream about wholeness, drawing it as a cereal packet, writing a haiku, working with memories that seem to express wholeness, or any technique that opens up the word for you and helps you to understand its meaning.

Here's my attempt:

> Wholeness is:
> Moving towards somewhere where it's good
>   for me to go;
> Feeling right with myself and others;
> Loving what I am and looking forward to
>   what I will be;
> A sense of understanding joy;
> A diminution of self;
> A laugh unbidden;
> A tickle of my pompous bone;
> Being undivided in purpose.

That works for me but I'm aware that some people prefer a more formal definition so in the spirit of being creatively challenged here's an attempt at that: Wholeness is being undivided in purpose, secure in oneself and with a positive attitude towards others.

Well, I said it was an attempt . . .

Now it's over to you to have a go – come up with your own working definition of wholeness.

Wholeness and perfection

Perfection is a town at the end of the line, it's a terminus, somewhere you arrive. Me, I like travelling. There's no creativity in perfection. How could there be? The place already has the perfect architecture, theatre, music, art and sculpture; and as for the people, well they're just . . . perfect.

This is why this chapter is called 'The creative path of wholeness', and not 'The creative path *to* wholeness'. To be whole we need, paradoxically, to be in need, not to be complete. Let me try to apply this paradox in an attempt to unpick it:

> I am very much enjoying writing this book. I've written only about 1,000 words of this chapter so far and although I will gain satisfaction from having written the rest I am, at present, delighted that it does not spring whole from my mind onto the page. We enjoy the joyous process of creation and for that we need blank sheets of paper, half-formed and unformed ideas; we need incompleteness; to be travelling, not arrived. Does this mean that we are not 'whole' or not experiencing wholeness as we write or dance or paint? Does it mean that when I lead creative workshops with their attendant dangers and uncertainties I am not whole? These creative acts certainly feel fulfilling but do not fill us up. They are energizing not sating, and this is why I write of 'The creative path *of* wholeness'. It is being on the path that is important; wholeness is not a town at the end of the line like perfection; rather it's the name of the road we walk.

Exercise 3 Charting wholeness

Take time out to make a mental audit of the last few days. Go through what you've done, including any times of quiet and thoughtfulness, and register your sense of wholeness in relation to your understanding of the term as explored in Exercise 2.

You might choose to write out your chart as in Table 1.

You'll see that I've included a rating, a mark out of ten. Quantifying wholeness in this way is perhaps rather trite but it can be useful to put numbers against quality issues even if they are somewhat imprecise. It's only for your own use so try using numbers in this way to see if it helps you to focus.

Table 1 Charting wholeness

Events of the last few days	Qualities of wholeness	Rating
Watching film on TV	Became wrapped up in it at certain points and so was very focused and unified but was also distracted by other things going on in the house.	6
3 hours writing	Became completely engrossed and felt that I did some good work, very satisfying.	10
Reading	Started a new book and quickly felt at home in it, became pleasantly involved.	7
Conversation with A	Seemed to get off on the wrong foot, felt A was unnecessarily critical and that I was too.	2
Ironing	Expected to drift off into a pleasant daydream, which is my usual way of choring, but phone kept ringing and had to switch focus and think about work.	4
Phone conversation with B	Nice surprise to hear from B as I thought she was away on holiday. Pleasant, mostly inconsequential chat.	6
Swimming	Relaxing. Time passed quickly as I was thinking about a project I'm looking forward to.	7
Later conversation with A	Both more relaxed but wary; felt able to communicate better. Holds out promise of improved relationship.	6

When you have your chart, think about it by asking the following questions:

- What kinds of activities give me the greatest sense of wholeness?
- What kinds of activities give me the least sense of wholeness?
- Are there any single activities that stand out as particularly positive?
- Are there any single activities that stand out as particularly negative?
- Is there anything I can do to increase the time I spend on positive activities?
- Can I do anything about the more negative activities, either to help me avoid them or to change what happens or how I view them?
- Has this exercise changed my understanding of wholeness?

It's worth doing these exercises several times to get a more complete picture. Many people find that the simple act of thinking about and then writing down their thoughts in this way is beneficial in itself. It helps you to gain perspective and not to feel swamped by the more negative aspects. It also encourages you to think about what you can change.

Know yourself

Having worked through the first three exercises you should:

- have found time for creative reflection;
- have some sense of what wholeness means for you;
- have gained some understanding of how you live in relation to your understanding of wholeness.

In your next creative sessions you're going to move on to one of the most important aspects of wholeness: knowing yourself. This is a big, in fact a never-ending, topic; not in a narcissistic way of being endlessly fascinated with oneself but in the sense that we are always changing. I can't tell you how long to spend on this or the exact course to follow but my suggestion, to get you started, is that you spend a week of creative thinking sessions, one per day on this important topic. This will be made up of five sessions with a sixth for reflection and consolidation (in effect, What have I learnt and what should I do next?); the seventh day is a day of rest! I can't proscribe the length of the sessions and, indeed, if you begin to enjoy and value this work you'll probably find that you stop thinking in terms of 'sessions' and simply work creatively whenever you can. As before, I think you'll achieve a lot in just ten minutes a day (although you won't be able to cover all the suggestions in each exercise in that time so apply your creative judgement and pick and choose, saving the others for a later time).

I suggest you start with the six-day plan below (Exercises 4 to 9) just to get you going and adapt/abandon it as you get into your stride. Some of my suggestions involve more than just thinking and you'll need to build in some time to do these or devise your own version that fits your lifestyle. After this week-long focus on 'Know yourself', I suggest you move on to the next section, 'Go beyond yourself' and the following headings, returning to 'Know yourself' at a later date. There are a variety of thinking and doing exercises and I suggest that you start each one with the relaxation into meditation programme as outlined in Chapter 3.

Exercise 4 What is a person?

1 Imagine that you have been asked to describe to some other being what it's like to be human, not what is a human being like (water, carbon, limbs, trunk, etc.), but what the experience of being a human being is. Think back to experiences you've had that you think help to reveal this difficult truth. Choose one experience and represent it in some way: picture it in your mind, depict it in art, prose or poetry.

2 Imagine that you are taking an examination in the subject, 'What is it like to be human?' What areas of questioning might be on the paper?

3 Prepare one part of your presentation (to the other beings) on 'What it's like to be human'. This might be a drawing, a speech, a piece of prose or even a dance.

Exercise 5 Where did I come from?

1 What are the 'sources' of you? Make a list. Here are some suggestions:
- My parents
- My birth family
- My environment
- Everything that's happened to me
- My marriage
- My married family
- My thoughts
- My reading
- My friends
- My sexuality
- God
- Natural selection
- The 'laws' of the universe

2 Choose one 'source' of 'you' and dwell on it, asking yourself questions such as:
   - How do I reflect the 'source' in the way that I behave?
   - Has the influence of this 'source' been mostly positive, negative or a mixture?
   - If I could speak to this source (as if it were a single entity), what would I say? Would my tone be one of criticism or thanks?
   - If the source could speak to me now, what would it say in answer to the question: What sort of person am I?

Exercise 6 The changing face

1 How have you changed during your lifetime? Imagine snapshots of yourself at different periods of your life. For each one consider:
   - How did I look?
   - What were my interests?
   - How was my personality different from today?

2 Now consider a much shorter period of time, say 24 or 12 hours. Are you the same person over this period? Is there a core 'you' or are you more of a conglomerate, made up of different manifestations of 'you' at different times?

3 Use framing techniques to help you consider these difficult questions:
   - If you were a colour in your earliest memory, what colour would you be?
   - And what colour would you be at age 7, 11, 16, 21 ... ?
   - If you were an animal when you first awoke this morning, what animal would you have been?
   - And what animal were you after breakfast, after lunch and now?

Exercise 7 The unfulfilled

1 Take some time to think about those areas where you have or had desires that were not fulfilled or have not yet been fulfilled.

Group them (either in your mind or by writing them on a chart) into categories:

- Things that I once wanted to achieve but am no longer interested in;
- Things that I once wanted to achieve that are now less important to me;
- Things that I once wanted to achieve and would still enjoy but now feel are impossible or inappropriate;
- Things that I once wanted to achieve and still want to achieve and that I believe are possible.

The third category may surprise some readers who have a philosophy that says, 'You can be whatever you want to be', but part of knowing ourselves is being realistic. Here's an example of what I mean: along with many other children of the space age, as a child I dreamed of going into space and walking on the moon. If I could do that today I would, but given the current state and cost of the technology and the fact that space travel is still a very risky business, I know that it's practically impossible that such tourism will be safely within my reach in my lifetime.

2 Focus on the final category, 'Things that I once wanted to achieve and still want to achieve and that I believe are possible', and prioritize the items in it. There are many ways you might do this, looking at what would be most fun, what would give the longest benefit, what would be best financially and so on, but I want to suggest that you should use your growing understanding of wholeness as the main criteria. Effectively you're asking: What do I

want to achieve that will contribute to my sense of wholeness?

I'm not suggesting that you spend too much time in this session trying to work out how you will achieve this goal or even take any steps towards it. That is not our focus here, but if you do identify something you'd like to achieve, make a note and come back to it later, applying the creative resources you've developed to help you take small practical steps towards your goal, as described in the final section of this chapter.

Exercise 8 The fulfilled – celebrate!

1 Have a party in your mind: think of all the positive things you achieved throughout your life. Think of the positive things you've achieved recently.

   Celebrate the miracle of life and consciousness, the fact that you are here, a living creative being.

2 Imagine yourself being interviewed just for being you on *Desert Island Discs*, *This Is Your Life*, or in a profile for a newspaper or magazine. Don't be embarrassed. No one else is hearing this so enjoy the fantasy. (Interestingly many people, me included, relish the idea of a fantasy like this more than the reality; you get all the fun with none of the embarrassment!)

3 Spread the party into your life for a day. Give yourself a treat just for being you. Some ways of doing this are:

   • Wear clothes that you particularly like and let them remind you all day of who and why you're celebrating.

   • Wear something like a flower, badge or piece of jewellery that will remind you that you're celebrating. It can be fun to wear something that no one else recognizes as special.

- Decorate your room or workspace. You can do this in a discreet way, just by adding a picture or some flowers or changing your computer wallpaper; or, if you feel like it, go for a full on decoration with balloons and streamers. Think in advance about what you'll say if people ask you why you're celebrating!
- Get in touch with some friends and arrange a drink or meal, you can celebrate being you and friendship at the same time.

Exercise 9 Evaluate

1 Take some time to go back over the week's discoveries and questions, using any evidence you have such as notes and drawings. Ask yourself: What have I learnt and what do I still need to work on? Use any of the creative ideas in this book to represent your ideas about yourself after this first week of exploration. For example:
- If I dreamed that I met myself, what would the dream be?
- Write a book-jacket blurb describing yourself as if you were a character in a novel.
- Write a film-trailer for your life story.
- Represent your discoveries in a free-form piece of artwork.
- Write a haiku encapsulating your sense of self.
2 Make a note of anything you've discovered that might lead to practical outcomes, things you can change or do, small steps or large. Take these ideas into your work in the section 'Practise creative living' below (p. 151).

Go beyond yourself

I suggest giving roughly the same amount of time (about a week of once-a-day creative work) to exploring the ideas in this section before moving on.

Exercise 10 Big sky

1 Seek out a starry night in a location far away from street lights if possible. This is much harder than you might think, certainly in the UK where light pollution denies us of one of the most important experiences that was a regular occurrence for previous generations. Recently in a quarry in Menorca (again) at midnight (don't ask) we looked up to see the Milky Way arching across the sky, something that one of our teenage children had never seen before.

As you look up, simply enjoy the spectacle and allow your mind to wonder at the distances and time involved. Recognize that some of the 'stars' you see are in fact collections of stars, and some are entire galaxies. Consider that the light you are seeing as you look at a star may have been travelling for millions of years and that the object you are looking at may no longer even exist. Reflect on the fact that most of the stars that you can see, you are actually looking at as they were before you were born.

2 If you can't find such a spot, go there in your mind using the meditation techniques in Chapter 3. You can do this either by taking into the meditation a mental picture of the actual night sky at the time (easily available from the Web, from stargazer computer programmes or from broadsheet newspapers), or by simply imagining a group of stars, and perhaps the moon and planets. You could also imagine the sky gradually darkening as night descends

and perhaps the odd shooting star as well. If you've ever been to a planetarium you'll have a rich source of imaginary pictures to draw on – if you haven't, perhaps you can schedule a trip . . .

3 Whether your view of the night sky is real or imaginary, reflect on how you are connected to what you see because it really is true that 'we are stardust'. All the atoms of which everything is made, including you and me, were formed in the creation and death of stars. You only exist because the stars you are looking at existed first. You can only think, and know that you think, because of the starry sky. How many other relationships will we discover between unimaginably distant celestial objects and their observers here on earth?

Exercise 11 Chain of humanity

1 Visit an old graveyard where there are tombstones going back centuries. Choose one and imagine the days, hours and seconds of that life. Try to grasp the idea that this was a person much like you who perhaps even stood where you are standing looking at the graves of their ancestors or other local people. Use this experience to help you gain perspective of your place as part of the human family – living, dead and yet to be born, both here and all over the world.

2 Think back through the generations of your family as far as you know them: your parents, their parents and so on. Think of the seed of you in your parents, their seed (which gave birth to your seed) in their parents and so on. Think of parental love and influence in the same way. This also means that the exercise is not limited to the biological line for those for whom this is important.

3 Choose a relative who has died, either someone you knew or

an imaginary version of some other ancestor. You could even make up a relative from way back in your family history. Hold an imaginary conversation with that person. Tell them about your life, its joys and difficulties. Be prepared to explain things – an ancestor might not know what an aeroplane is, or the ego or a washing machine . . . You can extend this by imagining what the relative would tell you if they talked about their life.

Exercise 12 Go wild

1 Go to the wildest, most remote location you know and spend some time there, trying to get some sense of how you, as a conscious being, fit into the landscape. Try to gain some sense of how it was formed, goes on and will go on without you. If you're feeling philosophical, you could ask whether its power and beauty could exist without people to perceive and label it.
2 As in the 'Big sky' exercise above, if you can't actually get to the place, go there in your mind.
3 What is the essence of this place for you? How does it make you feel and what qualities make it special in your mind? If you could bottle the essence of the place, what would you write on the label? How would you describe the place in a travel book? Is there a piece of music that matches the mood, feel and meaning of the place? If so, play it!

Exercise 13 Scale

1 Go on an imaginary journey using meditation techniques. Begin with an electron in orbit within an atom. Pull out to see the atom and imagine it forming a molecule that's part of your blood, then imagine the blood in your veins; pull out to a wider perspective to see your whole body, your

whole family, your town, country, world, the planets in
orbit around the sun, and so on, trying to move from
considering the smallest possible thing imaginable to the
largest scale possible, the whole universe. Good luck!

2 Consider these questions after the above meditation:

- Is a human being big or small?
- Does size have any meaning? (Not the same as 'Does size
  matter?'!)
- Which is bigger, the planet Jupiter or the mind that can
  ask this question?

Exercise 14 Divine

1 Turn your thoughts to God, beginning by thinking back
through your life, focusing on your beliefs at different
stages. Did you believe in God as a child? What did you
believe God was like in your earliest memories? When did
your ideas change? Can you chart a growing understanding
and a changing 'picture' of God? This could include
growing away from ideas of God and ceasing to believe, if
that is part of your divine history. End by thinking about
what you believe about God now.

2 What would you say if you could talk to God now? For
some people this will be meaningless because their answer
is that they do talk to God every day; for others it will be
meaningless because they are sure there is no God to talk to.
Whatever your views, step back and consider what you
would like to say to God if such a thing were possible.
Would you bring, hurt, distrust, anger, confusion, thanks-
giving, feelings of embarrassment . . . ?

Decide if you want to actually bring these things to God,
a God that you may not be sure of, whose existence you
doubt. If you do, take this thought into your prayer with

you: a good earthly parent wouldn't turn away their child because the child approached them hesitantly, unsure of their reaction; so if there is a God and God is like a good human parent it surely doesn't matter if you bring all sorts of uncertainties and even negativity with you . . .

I can't tell you how to pray, but one suggestion is that you treat it very much like meditation and start by telling God that this is what you've felt and thought about him or her over the years. Where it goes from there I leave to you . . . and God.

If you don't want to pray, for whatever reason, you can still do the meditation and use it to help you understand your current views about God and the effect ideas of the divine have had on you.

Exercise 15 Evaluate

1 Take some time to go back over the week's discoveries and questions, using any evidence you have, such as notes and drawings. Ask yourself: What have I learnt and what do I still need to work on? Use any of the creative ideas in this book to represent your findings after this week of exploration. For example:

 • Write a statement about your place in history.

 • Design the cover for a book about your family history. Give the book a title.

 • Draw, paint or imagine a picture entitled, 'We are stardust'.

 • On a sheet of paper write, 'I am connected to . . .' at the top; then fill it with words, images or both that show your connectedness to the universe, other people, history and the divine.

 • Write a prayer to say last thing at night or first thing in the morning.

2 Make a note of anything you've discovered that might lead
   to practical outcomes, things you can change or do, small
   steps or large. Take these ideas into your work in the
   section, 'Practise creative living' below (p. 151).

Learn to live with others

Learning to live with others is a vital part of walking the
creative path of wholeness. It is in relation to others that we
truly know ourselves and fulfil our potential, becoming more
than we could be if left to our own resources. It is harder to
learn to accommodate others than to simply please ourselves
but for this reason it leads to greater rewards, greater wholeness. You cannot truly know yourself until you do so in relation to others, but it is important to bring your understanding
of yourself from earlier in this chapter into your work here so
that you are aware, for example, of how your moods and atti-
tudes affect the way you see others.

Exercise 16 Who do you know?

1 Think about all the significant people in your life at the
   moment.
   • Who do you have responsibilities to?
   • Who do you look forward to seeing?
   • Who do you write to or email most often?
   • Who do you think about a lot?
   • Are there people who you would like to get to know
     better, people you would like to spend more time with?
   If appropriate, make a note and add spending time with
   these people to your action points for practising creative
   living at the end of this chapter.
2 Dig out your old photos and have a look back, thinking

about people you know now and those you used to know but have lost contact with. Be kind to yourself when you undertake this sort of exercise as you may find unhappy or bittersweet memories stirred up, particularly if people in the photos have since died or if the relationship is now more difficult than it was.

If appropriate, make a decision to get back in contact with old friends and acquaintances; you could try to trace them using Internet resources such as Friends Reunited (www.friendsreunited.com).

You'll need to do some more creative work if getting in touch with a particular person is difficult in any way, perhaps because of a previous close relationship or an estrangement. In these circumstances, use the ideas in this book to help you reflect on the situation, decide on the best course of action and build up your strength for the encounter. You'll find useful ideas in Chapter 2, 'The creative path of exploration – dreams, memories and fresh thinking', and Chapter 3, 'The creative path of spirituality, meditation and prayer', particularly the sections on frames and perspective.

Exercise 17 How do you respond?

1 Living with others isn't just about other people, it's also about you and how you respond to others. Choose someone close to you who you want to think about. If possible use the meditation techniques you've learnt to help you to focus. Think back to a fairly typical encounter, perhaps a phone conversation or a planning session or shopping together – whatever's appropriate to the relationship. Run through the event in your mind, trying to build up a detailed picture of what happened and what was said. Think

about where and how you both stood or sat, how you greeted each other, who was first to speak and so on.

Now focus on your responses to what the other person said. Link this to other times you've spent with that person. Can you see a pattern of responses? Are you stuck on some kind of track or in a narrow range of responses? Are you aware of how you treat this person or are you just responding on autopilot?

Run the scene through again in your mind and look for opportunities to react differently, perhaps more positively or less predictably. You're looking for ways to put some extra life into the relationship by breaking out of old habits. Try to avoid judging what the other person said or how they reacted – that's not something you can easily change whereas you can work on your own responses.

If appropriate, add this to your action points for the section, 'Practise creative living' below (p. 151).

2 Get into the habit, in certain situations, of setting a film camera running in your head so that you become aware of what you're saying and how you're behaving. This is not something you'll want to do all the time. It may be entirely inappropriate to treat intimate relationships in this way, but in work situations or any time when you feel you don't give of your best this can be a good way of reflecting on your behaviour and changing it for the better.

You're aiming to develop a sense of perspective so that you're able to respond to situations as if you're looking from outside at your own behaviour. If that sounds scary or too difficult, a good place to start is to run over things in your head just after they've happened; so, for example, you come out of a meeting and immediately (or when you have a moment's peace and quiet such as while travelling) run back over what happened. You may well be thinking that this is something you do all the time anyway but the essence of this exercise is to get into the habit of seeing things from a perspective outside yourself. So instead of thinking, as we so often do, 'If only I'd thought to say . . .' or 'She was really annoying me', learn to see yourself and your behaviour from outside so you think things like, 'I was distracted at the beginning, thinking about other things and M probably picked up on that' or 'I didn't need to stand up to make that point; I probably came over as a bit heavy.' You should also be kind to yourself, pointing out where you've acted positively, 'I really listened to B and began to change my view of her.'

Exercise 18 Someone else's shoes

1 Who are your heroes? Think about this and try to identify people who you look up to. They can be public figures or people known personally to you.

Choose one hero (I'm using the term to mean either male or female of course), and think about their special qualities. Why is that person a hero to you? If a third person were to write about why you've chosen that person, would they say it was because you are like or unlike your hero? In other words, does your hero reflect and amplify qualities that you have, or qualities that you wish you had?

One of my heroes is Harpo Marx. I love the scene in *Horsefeathers* where he's seen shovelling the professor's books into the fire (it sounds like nothing unless you know the film, so see it!). Something about his anarchic humour calls to me, representing, I think, a desire to be a free and perhaps outrageous spirit, to be anything but respectable. But Harpo was really a very gentle soul. Of all the Marx brothers, he lived life in the most relaxed fashion, doing his comedy (including a ground-breaking solo tour of Russia) and playing his harp. Unlike his more famous brother Groucho, he remained married to one person (Susan) and didn't allow the vagaries of Hollywood and the stock market to get to him. He seemed to have the knack of taking pleasure in the great gifts life had given him. So Harpo is a hero of mine, and in this case he represents many qualities that I'd like to have more of.

Do this exercise for yourself before moving on to the next part.

2 Imagine what it would be like to be your hero and try living in their shoes, thinking about how they would react to situations. Use meditation techniques to help you consider their qualities as above, then think through common situations you find yourself in and try to imagine how your hero would bring their qualities to bear.

One way of helping you to focus on this in daily life is to carry something that represents your hero or a particular quality. To make it more fun this could be in a kind of code so that it means nothing to anyone else. For example, we have an old East German 50 mark note from trips we made there when this was going 'behind the Iron Curtain'. That could remind me of Harpo *Marx* – not only because of the name but because of his trip 'behind the Iron Curtain'. Or to remind me of that relaxed quality I could carry an elastic band; a pen with no innards could remind me of the anarchic Harpo, and so on.

3 Develop the ability to see things from others' points of view and take this skill into your dealings with people. If you practise this you should be able to learn to empathize with others more in 'real time' (i.e. not when meditating after the event).

Start in a small way by monitoring your reactions to things people say and do, then immediately try to see it from their point of view.

Exercise 19 Learn to learn from others

1 There is wisdom, skill and knowledge all around you and yet, if you're anything like me, you tend to ignore a lot of it a lot of the time. Who do you know who's wise in some particular area? Who do you know who has a greater sensitivity to others than you do? Who do you know who has better people skills, is more organized or knows how to have more fun?

   Choose someone who has a quality you admire and appoint them your teacher for that subject. Start by learning from them by listening and watching with a focused mind, looking for clues as to how they approach the topic. Let's say you want to be better at running meetings and you've appointed Stella as your teacher. You'll probably be surprised how much you can learn if, the next time you're in a meeting with Stella, you decide to learn all you can about how she runs her meetings simply by observing her in action.

   Afterwards, take a few moments to reflect on what you've learnt and to apply it to yourself, adapting Stella's wisdom to your own situation and style.

2 Talk to your Stellas! Most people are flattered if you say quite openly that you admire something about them and would like to talk about it. You needn't go in with an attitude of hero worship or flattery as, with the wrong person, this may sound like flirting or lead them to be suspicious. The key is that you have something you want to understand better and they seem to have some wisdom in this area, so

it shouldn't be beyond your creative skills to come up with a way of talking to them about this. This can be terribly prosaic as in this extract from a conversation between me and another radio producer:

> Me: Yes, but you're well known for your skill in casting. I can never remember from one year to the next who played what and how good they were.
> Him: Thanks, I've actually managed to get some work just doing casting for TV and I really enjoy it.
> Me: You must have a good memory for faces and voices.
> Him: No. I've got a terrible memory. That's why I write down every actor I've worked with and what they did and some comments about them in this little book.
> Me: (feeling bloody stupid in a 'that's so obvious' kind of way) Oh, that's a good idea . . .

3 Seek out teachers. Identify areas that you want to work on and then keep a lookout for people who exemplify those skills. As well as proving useful in helping you to learn from others about those specific issues, this will do wonders for your social and 'networking' skills as you plan how to learn from your chosen teachers and how to engage them in conversation. If like me you're English, you may have a certain reserve about this kind of thing, feeling that you're somehow 'using people'. That's certainly one way of looking at it and you will obviously want to avoid making a nuisance of yourself but I believe that we need to take hold of the idea that we are all connected, none of us are islands, and in order to be whole we need to acknowledge this and be prepared to learn from each other. Besides, most people do like being asked about things they're good at and if you find that someone

really doesn't want to talk you can always go on to find another teacher.

4 One group of people who are rich in teachers are the elderly who, through their stories of how things used to be and their experience of living through change, can teach us a great deal. Recently, for example, I heard of childhood Sunday meals in a large family where there was no room in the oven to cook a joint and roast potatoes and so it was common practice to take the meat and potatoes in a roasting tray to the local baker who would cook several families' meals at once. The woman telling the story told how, as a child, she would be sent to collect the heavy dish of cooked food and would struggle home with it, being careful not to drop it. She would rest it on window sills on the journey and couldn't resist eating a roast potato every time she stopped.

You can enjoy this kind of thing as a charming story but you can also learn from it, perhaps asking your 'teacher' about community-sharing in those days and what we might learn from it today. You can also think about this story as a metaphor, perhaps for a greener way of living or as a parable of using our gifts for the good of all.

Exercise 20 Celebrate relationships

1 Like most of us you probably take your relationships for granted most of the time. It's only when things go wrong, when the friend has moved away or if they have died that we realize how important they were to us.

Take time to celebrate your important relationships now. Think about all the people you are still in contact with and, one by one, think about why this person is special to you and what they uniquely bring into your life.

One way of doing this is to think of your friends and

special relationships as like the parts of a meal so you might say something like:

> Samira is when I wake up in the morning and look forward to eating a special meal that evening; she is bright, effervescent, rarely down and full of life.
>
> Don is like the plate that the meal is served on; I don't think of him often but when I need him he's always there, solid, reliable and supportive of others.
>
> Sally is a good wine, which as soon as you taste it puts you in a good mood; she's the life and soul of the party and I always feel comfortable and at home when I'm with her . . .

. . . and so on. Have some fun thinking about and celebrating your friends in this way.

2 Other metaphors for relationships are:
   - Thinking about your friends and special relationships as modern 'Knights of the Round Table', each with their own special qualities to bring to the kingdom.
   - Giving each friend a short phrase tagged onto their name such as Tim the meticulous, hilarious Hilary, rock-solid Sanjeev, and so on.
   - Casting your friends in films. Which of your friends would play Citizen Kane or Robin Hood or Joan of Arc?

3 You can apply any of these exercises to friends and loved ones with whom you are no longer in contact, including those who have died. How do you remember them and can you call on their special qualities to help you now?

Exercise 21 Evaluate

1 Take some time to go back over the week's discoveries and questions, using any evidence you have such as notes and drawings. Ask yourself: What have I learnt and what do I still need to work on? Use any of the creative ideas in this book to represent your findings after this week of exploration. For example:

- Write a letter to a special friend telling them why they are important to you. You can do this actually to send to the person or just for yourself if you prefer.
- Draw reminders about your friends' special qualities against their names in your address book.
- Write an imaginary school report on your attempts to learn from others.
- Draw a poster for a film, based on one of your important relationships, illustrating events that seem pivotal to you.

2 Make a note of anything you've discovered that might lead to practical outcomes, things you can change or do, small steps or large. Take these ideas into your work in the next and final section of this book.

Practise creative living

What have you learnt about yourself and others over the three weeks of looking at:

- Knowing yourself;
- Going beyond yourself;
- Learning to live with others?

Before returning to think further about any of these, it's time to make sure that you put some of your thinking into creative action because one of the main purposes of this book, and of this chapter in particular, is to focus on changes that we can make, not just to how we think but to how we act.

From day six of each of the three weeks of creative work you should have some practical ideas, many of which you may have put into action already. Some examples might be:

- Find more time to work creatively.
- Redefine your definition of wholeness.
- Achieve some goals identified in Exercise 7.
- Find the space to go to special places more.
- Read more poems/novels/philosophy/spiritual writings.
- Make more time for a hobby.
- Develop artistic skills.
- Write more.
- Make more time for and discover new music.
- Explore a religious faith.
- Meditate more.
- Pray once a day.
- Get in touch with . . .
- Make more time for . . .
- Learn from others.
- Learn to listen.
- Become more self-aware.
- Break repeating patterns in relationships.
- See things from others' points of view.
- Learn from and emulate your heroes.

Remember that this list is just to give you a wide range of possibilities. Hopefully you won't have anything like as many

things to work on but even so your list could be quite daunt-
ing. It's best not to think of the number of things you have to
do as if it's a list of requirements like revising for an exam. Try
instead to see it as representing opportunities. Look at your list
and prioritize those areas that you want to work on first. By
now you should have many creative possibilities to help you
think through this process if the priority is not immediately
clear. You could, for example, use meditation techniques to
help you imagine different futures that will result if you deal
with certain issues. You might group your ideas under different headings or consider how they relate to larger life goals.

However you work on your priorities, choose just one thing
that you want to work on for now and use your creative skills
to break it down into small, achievable steps. For example,
'Make more time for and discover new music' doesn't require
you to go to lots of concerts. It could just be a question of
tuning the car radio to a different station occasionally or
making a short detour to a music store next time you go shopping. Taking 'Learn from and emulate your heroes', you could
simply take a first step of writing a sentence that describes
how you hope to change your behaviour or what you want to
achieve. A longer version of this is to write a letter to yourself
to be opened in one month's time (or whatever time period is
appropriate for the changes you want to make), which set out
in more detail what you hope will have happened.

The key with putting any creative change into practice is to
take it one small step at a time, not to overburden yourself
and, most importantly, not to set yourself up for failure.

We are nearly at the end of our creative journey together
now but hopefully you are just at the beginning. The ideas in
this chapter do not represent a four-week course that you
complete, but inspiration for devising your own creative disci-

pline, so your next stage is to plan how you will continue to work. This is most important because if you don't make time for more thinking, more creative responses and more planning, you'll find that creativity will get squeezed out of your busy life. It does take effort to examine your philosophy, your ideas about yourself and your relationship with others and it is all too easy to lose your focus. I suggest that you look back over the book and perhaps reread any sections that you feel might inspire you afresh. You can also look for other books that offer creative ideas and feed them into your thinking. Bring to the process your ideas for the areas in your life that you need to concentrate on next and make some plans to continue your creative cycle. Don't be discouraged if you feel that you're not 'getting there'. Remember we're not going to a town called perfection, we're on a creative path of wholeness. Enjoy the journey.